HE'S A KEEPER, I'M A TOSSER

Other books by Carole Achterhof:

**NEVER TRUST A SIZE THREE
(ISBN 0-9625940-0-8)**

**POTATO CHIPS ARE VEGETABLES
(ISBN 0-9625940-1-6)**

**LIFE WITH A CHANNEL SURFER
(ISBN 0-9625940-2-4)**

HE'S A KEEPER, I'M A TOSSER

**Written and Illustrated by
CAROLE ACHTERHOF**

Cover design by LORI NISSEN

Bare Bone Books
Spirit Lake, IA 51360

Dedicated to Roger -
my best friend, my husband for 36 years,
and my favorite keeper.

Bare Bones Books
Rural Route 9061
Spirit Lake, IA 51360

Copyright © 1998 by Carole Achterhof

Library of Congress Catalog Card number: 98-92724
ISBN 0-9625940-3-2

Printed in the United States

First Printing

TABLE OF CONTENTS

Tossers And Keepers	7
The Garage Sale	9
Priceless Blue Jeans	11
Chocolate Diets - Too Good To Be True	13
Personal Lie Detectors	15
My Short Life As A Car Pooler	18
Life After Caffeine	20
The Coupon Clipper	22
Tonight's Menu: Road Kill	24
The Perils Of Map Folding	27
A Sure Cure For Garden Guilt	29
The Most Expensive Wedding	31
Post-Natal Insurance Blues	33
My Introduction To Computers	35
Ed And Bill Find The Cure For Acne	37
The Queen Of Clubs	39
Take-Out Dining	41
Exciting Driver's Training Update	43
Is it Chicken Or Pheasant?	45
Do-It-Yourself Coffins	47
We Become Politically Correct	49
Luxury Hotel Suites	51
Chain Letter Anguish	53
Please Pass The Salicylates	55
Weather Forecasters	57
Why Midwesterners Never Sleep	59
Thoughts Before The '96 Summer Olympics	61
Coupon Mania	64
South Dakota's Toe Service	66
My Sweepstakes Friends	68
My New Age Sister	70
Lost In Rural Space	72
Convenience Stores	75
All You Need To Know About Golf	77
Parenthood - A Moving Experience	79
The Magnificent Tomato Obsession	81
Mummifying Mom	83
Our Guest, The Computer	85
Hunger Awareness Month	87
The Body - Mass Index Is Explained	89
Cleaning The Refrigerator	91
A Giant Jump For Mankind	93
The Complications Of Retirement	95
Hang Around After You're Gone	97
The Six Stages Of Christmas	99
Snow Shoveling Precautions	101
Good Intentions	103

To Tip Or Not To Tip	105
Ice Fishermen: Our Next Astronauts	108
Blizzard Braggadocio	110
Promiscuous Fishing	113
The Tree-Cutting Chromosome	115
Charter Plane Trips	117
The Downside Of Cloning Ourselves	119
Sound Advice For Young Adults	121
The Deadly Mongoose	123
White House Guests - Who Cares?	125
Winter Amnesia	127
Lifestyles Of The Rich And Not So Rich	129
How To Handle Overdue Letters	131
My Time With The Phone Psychic	133
Gardening Blues	135
The Diet Backlash Movement	137
Surprise Weddings	139
The Beetle Makes a Comeback	141
The Great Spaghetti Sauce Threat	143
A Sow By Any Other Name	145
The New Villains	147
Trips Out Of This World	149
Our Worst Fears	151
Let's Export Baseball Caps	153
A Guide To Home Weddings	155
Mice Invasions	157
The New, Improved $50 Bills	160
Eating Becomes An Art	162
Going Nowhere For $80,000	164
A Pedicurist For Cows	166
Effects Of El Nino	168
The Cookie Baking Contest	170
Computerized Grave Markers	173
The Advantages Of Snail Mail	175
Realism And Barbie Dolls	177
Salt, Fats And Sugar: Back To The Basics	179
New Year's Resolutions	182
Leona Sells Her House	184
The Associated Press Vendetta	186
Bad Advice From Our Elders	188
Bad-Mouthing The Food On Our Tables	190
The Scrabble Competition	192
Hobbledehoy Names	194
Advice For New Parents	196

Tossers and Keepers

It may be true that a fool and his money are easily parted. Unfortunately, the same can't be said about some people and their unused items in closets, basements and attics.

During the past few weeks it has become painfully clear to me that the world is divided into tossers and keepers. I also realize that ours is a mixed marriage. Although we may agree on everything else, from politics in the Middle East to whether or not Willard Scott looks better with a hairpiece, he's a keeper and I'm a tosser.

We're going to have a garage sale and I must admit that we're spending more time discussing the relative merits of junk than we once gave to whether or not to have another baby.

In fact, preparing for a garage sale takes up as much time as a full-term pregnancy. The only difference is that garage sales require several months of labor and they produce little or no glow. The closest I came to having a glow was when I moved too many boxes marked "miscellaneous" from one side of the garage to another.

Garage sales must be much easier for married couples who share similar philosophies about tossing and keeping. While I maintain that anything not used during the past three decades isn't worth storing, he views things quite differently. Considering the fact that he wasn't even a gleam in his father's eye during the Great Depression, I find that very remarkable.

The chasm between keepers and tossers becomes even wider when news programs tell about valuable Picassos found in people's basements or someone buying an item for a few cents at a garage sale and later selling it for thousands of dollars.

Even though there's a greater chance of being hit by lightning or finding the Publishers Clearing House people at the front door, those stories only serve to give false hopes to keepers.

Whether it's an electric frying pan without a heating element or a food blender without a blade, keepers tend to view broken appliances with the eye of a faith-healer. With a little dab of glue here and an extra part there, the appliances, like Lazarus, will rise from the dead.

When they reluctantly do part with items for a garage sale, keepers also tend to inflate prices. It doesn't seem unreasonable at all to charge $5 for a Tupperware lid, long separated from the bowl which melted in the dishwasher.

Perhaps I should be grateful to be married to a keeper. It's somewhat reassuring to know that even if I lose my shape, or even land up with missing parts, he will keep me around.

The Garage Sale

A large group of people showed up at our house last weekend. Judging from the cars clogging our driveway and the other vehicles parked along the roadside, a casual observer might have assumed we were having the social event of the season.

As our guests elbowed their way through the crowd, snippets of their conversations could be heard above the others. Two women huddled together in a corner, discussing my wardrobe.

"Can you imagine wearing that?" one asked. The other woman shook her head in disbelief.

I kept glancing at my watch, wondering when the event would finally end.

"Wonder how much they originally paid for this," mused one man, picking up a wooden cigar box.

"I dunno," answered his companion. "I can tell you one thing. I wouldn't give a dime for it."

Dinner plates were turned over in their hands as our guests tried to determine the names of the manufacturers. Not a single item escaped their scrutiny.

In other parts of the country what was going on at our house might have been called a party or a family reunion. In our neck of the woods, it's called a garage sale.

As I sat at the makeshift sales counter, a folding table with three functional legs and a fourth which threatened to collapse at any moment, I began thinking about the nature of garage sales. Selling plastic sandwich bags filled with seashells and unmatched drinking glasses gives a person a certain philosophical edge.

We live in a time when privacy is viewed as a precious commodity. We have Caller IDs on our telephones and we draw our drapes at night, so people won't see us doing unthinkable activities such as eating microwave popcorn and staring at a flickering television screen. Even if we were taken prisoner in a warlike situation, we would refuse to reveal how much we paid for our last car, our actual weights or our true clothing sizes. We jealously guard our privacy.

Garage sales are a different matter. We place classified ads in newspapers and put up signs, all listing our address and in some cases, our phone numbers. For the sake of selling a set of kitchen canisters for 25 cents or used golf balls for a nickel, we open our doors to complete strangers and allow them to criticize our worthless purchases from the past.

We sell items for a fraction of their original cost and we give the impression that our livelihoods depend on the sales.

A young visitor to our home recently asked me, "Why do you keep all of these empty bread bags in your kitchen drawer?"

Without much success, I tried to explain about the aftershocks of the Great Depression and how nothing should be thrown away that can possibly be used.

We either store those items in hopes of using them at a later date or we sell them at a garage sale. Had I not sold those 100 bread bags for a dime at the garage sale, I could have become a bonafide bag lady.

Priceless Blue Jeans

The secret to a successful life apparently is knowing what to keep and what to throw away. Keepers often have the edge.

That truth became painfully clear a few weeks ago when my husband found a postcard in the mailbox addressed to "Occupant". It read, "Spring Cleaning? Clean out your attic and barn! There is money in grandpa's old jeans!"

The card further described vintage jeans, now inflated to several times their original price. Pre-1950 Levi's are now worth up to $750, pre-1970 Wranglers are worth $200 and Levi Buckle Back Pants are commanding up to $1000.

As he dropped the card on the kitchen counter with the rest of the mail, he didn't say a word, but his eyes asked, "Did you throw those jeans away?"

He didn't ask because he already knew. The jeans had been thrown out ages ago, along with the Nehru jackets, the Buddy Holly records, dried-up corsages from high school proms and baby clothes.

As I see it, many people cling zealously to the philosophies of tosserism and keeperism. Pushed to the extremes, neither group is very rational. Tossers attempt to keep their surroundings pristine, orderly and minimal. Their counterparts seem only happy when they're surrounded by seemingly useless clutter.

Keepers unite under the motto, "Waste Not, Want Not." Given their way, there would be no need for landfills or trash cans.

"Who threw away this perfectly good cereal box?"

"That's not a rag. That's my favorite shirt!"

"Throwing away this pail of rusty nails is like throwing away money."

Keepers' lifestyles are fulfilled when a piece of junk they've salvaged can be used for some other purpose several years down the road. For example, a door handle from a '59 Pontiac can handily replace a broken knob on a kitchen cupboard.

The ends of keepers' lives are usually abysmal. They often include lying dead and undiscovered for weeks and having bulldozers level their homes, which are filled to the rafters with old magazines and newspapers.

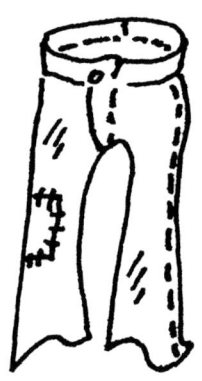

On the flip side, tossers follow the motto, "If you don't use it, lose it."

"Hey! What's this half-loaf of bread doing here? If you're not going to eat it, I'm throwing it away."

"When was the last time we actually sat in the shade of that tree? Let's chop it down!'

"I ask you, do we REALLY need this cat?"

The postcard about used blue jeans represents a real setback for tossers everywhere. Meanwhile, keepers have an excellent reason to either rejoice or commiserate.

Chocolate Diets –
Too Good To Be True

There are good diets and bad diets. However, the diet sent to me this week by an anonymous reader in St. Louis Park, MN, seems doomed from the very start. I'm no stranger to diets. In fact, I'm so good at dieting that I've lost 6,000 pounds over the past 20 years. On one diet plan, I drank so much water that the water meter in our basement vibrated off the wall and our town experienced an unusual water shortage.

Another diet required me to eat all of the grapefruit within a 50 mile radius of my home. Although the diet met with short-lived success, it took much longer for my lips to lose their permanent pucker.

One dismal diet plan offered synthetic food, which looked like real food but tasted like corrugated cardboard. The real pitfall of the diet was that soon everything, from sheetrock to library paste, looked good enough to eat.

The new diet is based on the premise that you can keep your body from knowing it's on a diet. The plan sounds simple: on alternating days, a dieter eats two chocolate wafers every two hours and nothing else. On the other days, you can eat anything you want.

"Eat as you would when you're not dieting!" proclaims the brochure.

They must be kidding. Apparently the founders of the diet have never met someone with my grazing habits. They must have some of us confused with people who limit themselves to three meals a day. If I had that much restraint, I wouldn't need to diet.

Actually, I'm a reasonable eater until 4:00 p.m. rolls around. I eat a modest breakfast (toast and coffee) and a well-balanced lunch (that is to say, all the food that can be balanced on a cafeteria tray at work).

Once I return home, however, I bear a close resemblance to something from a B-grade movie – perhaps "The Creature Who Ate Las Vegas". Wandering from cupboard to cupboard, refrigerator shelf to refrigerator shelf, I devour everything in sight. If it doesn't carry a poison label or move about on its own free will, it's fair game.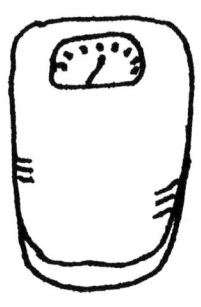

The grazing stage of my day lasts until bedtime. By that time I'm too tired to eat. Tearing open potato chip bags, reaching for forks and spoons and constantly shuffling around the kitchen can be an exhausting regimen.

If the chocolate wafer plan is followed to the letter, it would be possible to take in 30,000 calories every other day. Some diet plans are simply too good to be true.

Personal Lie Detectors

If you are already set up with a computer system and have $149 to spare, the truth may be yours.

Makh-Shevet, a small Israeli high-technology company, claims that its new CD-ROM software can detect whether the person on the other end of the phone line is under stress, fudging an answer or lying. The new software, Truster, can be installed on a Windows 95 or Windows NT computer and then linked to a nearby telephone.

Much less expensive than the voice-stress analyzers which cost law enforcement people $5,000 to $8,000 or having your mother move in so she can screen your callers, Truster measures changes in voice frequency. According to the system, if a voice alters considerably during a phone conversation, truth is on rather shaky ground.

That could be a problem. Suppose you're handed a quadruple cappuccino instead of the usual single at your favorite coffee shop on the way to work. With enough caffeine anyone would sound like a psychopathic liar.

Problems could also arise if you're standing in a phone booth, dialing a number, when you're suddenly attacked by a rabid skunk. Imagine the dubious credibility of a 15-year-old boy who can at one minute sound like a grizzly coal miner and the next minute sound like his younger sister.

In two particular instances, doing business over the phone, rather than in person, would eliminate needless headaches:

"Thanks so much for this car repair estimate, but could you call me at home so we can discuss what it really will cost?"
"I would really like to buy this used car, but could you call me at home? Let's talk more about the odometer."
Truster would also reveal the falsehoods underlying the following telephone statements:
It was the best first date I've ever had. I'll call you again soon. I promise.
The check is in the mail.
You haven't received my letters? Well, you know how the post office is...
Of course I love you!
If you switch to our long-distance company, the savings will surprise you.
You really should meet Albert. He's a prince of a guy!
Before long we should expect to hear about Truster II, which will display the caller's real thoughts on computer screens while they say something else:
The 2,000 photos you sent me of your new grandchild were priceless! (Now I know why some animals eat their young!)
Oh, are you still awake, Mom? I'll be coming home a little late because I studied so long at the library. (That's right, isn't it? We do have a public library in our town, don't we?)
You looked great when I saw you today! Did you lose weight? (Have you thought about applying for your own Zip Code?)
Thank you again for inviting us for dinner at your home. The food was absolutely wonderful! (As I was

telling my husband after we had our stomachs pumped at the hospital on our way home, that food was something else.)

With the introduction of Truster, we should also consider what we should do when the tables are turned and we are the ones being secretly Trusterized. Perhaps the best advice for such a situation was given by Mark Twain, who noted, "When in doubt, tell the truth."

My Short Life As A Car Pooler

It's easier to read facts than to face them.

Long before I began car pooling to work with my husband in 1994, I came across some startling statistics — the average married couple spends only 20 minutes a week in meaningful conversation.

When we moved to a new home earlier that year, we realized the change would mean a one-hour commute to our old jobs. Even though we knew our commuting plans would result in trading off certain luxuries in life — namely sleep and breathing — we faced the prospect with unbridled enthusiasm.

Actually we felt that way only once before. When we were first married we had twenty dollars between us, but we were confident that amount would keep us fed for at least a year.

So it was with the same hope we faced car pooling. If nothing else we would be beating the odds and having 10 uninterrupted hours a week of meaningful conversation.

The first week wasn't a disappointment. The hours and miles flew by as we drove under spectacular sunrises and breath-taking sunsets. As we sipped coffee from matching travel mugs, our conversations were lively and spirited.

Within the first five days we knew each other's position on almost every topic under the sun — from a possible invasion of Haiti to the complications of a national health care plan. As we dodged the day-glo orange barriers of road repairs, we discussed books, movies and a gamut of other interesting subjects.

By the second week, some of the thrill was obviously missing. He began forgetting the car keys and I began spilling coffee on my clothes. Although there were still plenty of topics left unresolved but touched upon from time to time, he began listening to the radio and I began reading the newspaper.

The trips seemed longer during the third week. Our scintillating conversations had been reduced to monosyllables, mostly "Uh huh" and "Hmmmm." Within an amazing three weeks, we had gone from best-selling books and Steven Spielberg to grunts and groans. In the great scheme of things, it appeared the fine art of conversation had been set back a couple thousand years. Our guttural noises sounded like the soundtrack from the old Raquel Welch movie, "One Million Years B.C."

If the trend continued, I suspected that we would soon feel more comfortable hanging by our heels from trees and peeling bananas than sharing the front seat of a car.

Life After Caffeine

In a study of caffeine addiction, Johns Hopkins scientists have boiled down a list of withdrawal symptoms. The grounds for addiction include temporary headaches, lethargy and depression.  One of the surprising conclusions of the study is that in spite of these withdrawal symptoms, caffeine isn't associated with serious health risks.

The longest week of my life occurred when I once decided to switch from leaded to unleaded coffee. In addition to the symptoms listed above, my hands and legs shook like ingredients in a blender and I gave serious thought to driving over the edge of a cliff. The only things that saved me were returning to caffeine and living in a relatively flat area of the country.

As a public service to those considering quitting caffeine, I offer the following list of withdrawal symptoms. You know you've been addicted to caffeine when:

You can understand why hamsters and gerbils eat their young.

You seriously consider taking an afternoon nap at eight in the morning.

You can't write because pencils and pens keep breaking in half as you hold them.

Because you're hands are so shaky, your lipstick is applied from ear to ear.

Your voice quivers so much when you talk that people think you're doing an imitation of Katherine Hepburn.

You completely demolish three bicycles and an extension ladder while backing the car out of the garage. What's more, you don't care.

You prepare a shake and bake chicken dinner without intending to do so.

You find yourself ripping coffee ads out of magazines and eating them.

You answer the phone with "Wadda you want?" or you don't answer the pone at all because you think the ringing is in your ears.

During one of your many daytime lapses into the unknown you dream about swimming in a pool filled with espresso.

You fall asleep at the computer at work and wake up to discover you've printed out 20 pages of X's.

When people ask "How are you?" you really tell them.

While getting ready for work in the morning, you set the bowl of instant oatmeal on the back porch and microwave your cat.

You cry during television commercials.

And finally, the ultimate withdrawal symptom - you don't really care which company gets your long-distance telephone business.

The Coupon Clipper

I shopped behind my worst dream this week. Actually, she was a grocery store nightmare.

Before I describe the woman to you, understand that I have nothing against saving money while shopping for groceries. Given the alternative of holding up a bank for marshmallow and breakfast cereal money, being frugal is the nobler of the two options.

As usual, I picked that particular checkout lane because it had the least number of people. Also as usual, it turned out to be the slowest line and it seemed at one point that I would miss two meals and go through my entire change of life while standing there.

After her groceries had been tallied up, the woman pulled out a bulging packet of cents-off coupons. Of all different shapes and colors, the great quantity of coupons clearly dated back to at least 1956. Slowly and methodically, the woman pulled out one coupon and then another.

As I glanced at my watch impatiently, I calculated that my family's E.T.O.E. (Estimated Time of Eating) would be sometime after the late night news. It was too late to move my cart to another lane - at least four carts were clustered behind mine.

By the time she had rifled through her last 4,000th coupon, the general agitation in our line would have registered at least 8.5 on the Richter Scale. Except for the confusion created by the store's promotion, a turkey card, we would have been free and clear.

Seemingly unaffected by the daggers of disgust aimed in her direction, disgust normally reserved for serial killers and people who neglect to return overdue video rentals, she noticed that her total cost for groceries gave her the final punches for her free turkey card.

"I'll take my turkey now," she announced to the cashier. "Where are they?"

"In the back of the store," wearily responded the cashier, and by the tone of her voice I could tell 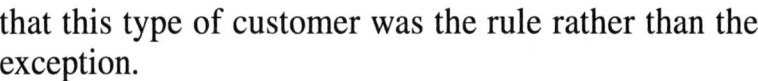 that this type of customer was the rule rather than the exception.

Hurdling over the seven or eight carts now behind her and tackling a rack of National Enquirers which stood in her path, the woman headed for the meat department, a good football-field distance away. She returned what seemed like several hours later, proudly waving the frozen turkey over her head as if it were the game ball.

"Will there be anything else?" sweetly asked the cashier of the woman, who was now frantically searching every pocket of her purse for her checkbook.

"As a matter of fact, there is," answered the woman. "I'd like two lottery cards."

A general groan went up from the crowd of disgruntled shoppers, who by this time felt as though they were in grocery store purgatory. Except for the fact that most shoppers don't carry hanging ropes in their purses, the woman would have been history.

What seemed like eons later, the cards had been scratched, the bill had been paid and the woman was merrily off on her way. It may have been my imagination, but as she exited through the door, I was certain I could hear voices singing Handel's "Hallelujah Chorus."

Tonight's Menu: Road Kill

Do you remember the Road Kill Cafe T-shirts that were all the rage a few years ago? With the passage of time, it's safe to assume that most of those shirts are now serving as dusting and polishing rags.

It now appears that life is imitating art, or at least the tongue-in-cheek cafe menus printed on the shirts. Last month, the West Virginia Senate was expected to pass a bill legalizing the eating of road kill.

Road kill is a term not easily understood by city dwellers, who must content themselves with slamming their cars into tall buildings, shopping carts left in parking lots and unwary pedestrians. However, in the rural areas of our country, where wild animals outnumber humans on the highways, certain unpleasantries are unavoidable.

"This is not a joke," noted Leonard Anderson, a state senator from West Virginia. He hopes that encouraging drivers to dine on the creatures they accidentally run over will reduce the cost of having game wardens dispose of the carcasses. His state has at least 40,000 animal-car collisions each year, and current law permits motorists to keep road kill only if they contact authorities, which "can take hours, and the meat is spoiled by then."

The senator added, "It's a serious problem."

If car bumper buffets catch on, creative cooks in the senator's state will soon be knee-deep in raccoon ragout, venison vichyssoise, pheasant fritters and squirrel surprise hot dishes. They will quickly spread the word that any wild animal – a snapping turtle, a snake, a gopher or a wild dog – can be smothered in cream of mushroom soup and the results will invariably taste like chicken.

However, there's always a downside to any new bill. The possibility exists that drivers will interpret the term "road kill" as meaning any animal within 500 yards of their cars and they will be reporting home with their cellular phones.

"Clean out the deep freezer, honey. I've loaded up the backseat with three pigs, a cow and three stray farm cats!"

Colliding with a deer will be a cause for celebration, far outweighing the misery of filling out countless car insurance forms.

"What a great day! I hit three deer on my way to work!"

Before they replace the tire jacks in their car trunks with shovels and shish kabob skewers, West Virginia drivers should be given three pieces of advice:

If the meat you find on the highway has black fur with a white stripe running the length of the animal, no amount of cream of mushroom soup will make it edible.

If you can no longer identify the animal, don't eat the meat.

Out of respect for human-pet relationships, don't eat any meat still attached to a collar and name tag.

A similar road kill bill in Minnesota would have certainly changed a true story told by a friend of ours in Duluth. While he was traveling on a deserted highway early one morning in northern Minnesota, his car fatally struck a bear.

His car also sustained heavy damage and while filling out his accident claim form for the insurance company, our friend noted that his car has struck a bear.

A few weeks later, the insurance company, based in a large city, wrote back with a simple request, "Please give us the current address of Mr. A. Bear."

With a road kill bill similar to the one being considered in West Virginia, our friend could have responded, "He doesn't live around here anymore. We ate him."

The Perils Of Map Folding

The person who designed folding road maps was undoubtedly the same person who came up with the idea for the Rubik's Cube and programming VCRs. Trying to refold a road map in some logical order among its 106 creases is about as easy as doing brain surgery.

As they set off for summer vacations, families across the country are sure to discover that people are basically divided into two groups: those who believe maps can be refolded into their original shapes and those who don't.

I belong to the latter group. Even though our car doesn't have an airbag on the front seat passenger's side, I feel confident that at the right moment the glove compartment will pop open and cushion the passenger with an explosion of misfolded road maps.

Because we never throw away maps — many of them show 30-year-old interstate highways as dotted lines due for completion — one entire closet shelf also holds an ample supply. The closet, which doubles as a burglar alarm, would bury an unsuspecting thief in an avalanche of maps dating back to the Lewis and Clark expedition.

The latest issue of the San Anselmo, CA, recreation course catalog includes: "Map Folding. Learn to fold a map like a pro. Tired of having a messy glove box? Fed up with having your maps turned inside out, so you have to go through all of them to find the one you want?...No extra fee for international maps."

As it turns out, the course listing was simply a way

to find out if people were reading their catalog. Without realizing it, they had actually thought of a course really worth taking and they consequently gave false hopes to countless readers.

I'm married to a map folder. Although that particular virtue is often overlooked during most of the year, it's not until we take a car trip that his views on map-folding become a topic of conversation. After traveling through five or six states and the same number of maps, he is usually quick to ask, "Is that any way to fold a map?" 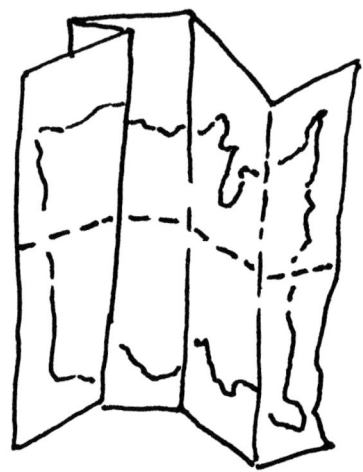 Given my unorthodox approach to map-folding, he might as well be asking, "Is that any way to solve a geometric equation?"

Except for missing shoulder straps, his maps look like neatly pleated accordions. Mine, on the other hand, look like crushed wads of paper destined for a wastebasket.

Refolding a map correctly requires infinite patience and several years of lessons in origami, the fine art of Japanese paper folding. My maps may be crushed and smashed and creased in places that have never been creased before, but when it comes to map folding, I honestly don't give a rip.

A Sure Cure For Garden Guilt

The residents of Bunol, Spain, may have come up with the cure for "gardening guilt".

Gardening guilt is the result of turning one's back on a healthy garden while it's still producing and weeks before the first killing frost. It means standing in a patch of ripening tomatoes, waving a hoe towards the heavens and shouting, "Enough is enough! I can't take this anymore!"

Refusing to process one more jar of pickle relish means rejecting all of the advice passed down to us since childhood — "Waste not, want not" and "Clean up your plate". Ignoring a garden in the early fall runs counter to every precept we've been taught about starving children in Asia and the dreaded words, "I don't care if you don't like dilled beans. I've worked my fingers to the bones canning 4,000 quarts and you're going to enjoy them!"

Gardening guilt follows fast on the heels of other emotions, most notably pride, satisfaction and greed. Few satisfactions in life can rival picking the first ripe tomato from a garden and devouring it immediately.

Fortunately or unfortunately, depending upon your perspective, picking the first tomato is much like plucking a first gray hair. The first tomato is replaced by two and those two are eventually replaced by 100. After eating enough bacon, lettuce and tomato sandwiches and canning enough spaghetti sauce, chili sauce and stewed tomatoes to feed most of the western hemisphere, we tend to become fickle.

While any tomato is acceptable at first, we eventually become tomato connoisseurs. As the weeks slip by, tomatoes with ground spots and those that aren't perfectly symmetrical are virtually ignored.

For that reason we might consider following the Spanish solution to garden overproduction. Recently, for the 51st year, over 20,000 potential tomato-tossers invaded the tiny town, population 9,215, and pelted each other with more than 100 tons of ripe tomatoes.

The "tomatina" tomato fight ranks right up there with the running of the bulls at Pamplona. Bunol is definitely classier than another small Spanish town where celebrators walk barefoot across hot coals while carrying people on their backs.

Actually, small towns in our country could follow suit and at the same time boost sagging rural economies. Unlike Bunol, where only olives, oranges and figs are grown and the tomatoes must be shipped in, we are surrounded by countless gardens like mine, brimming with overripe tomatoes. You say tomato. I say tourism.

The Most Expensive Wedding

Parents of prospective brides in this country should count their blessings. In order to keep up with the Smiths and the Joneses, they are only required to pay for a wedding by taking out a second mortgage on their home, selling their blood and living in abject poverty for several years.

The situation isn't as easy in India, where parents of brides must follow the recent example set by two well-known families, the Jayarams and the Ganesans. The bridegroom is the foster son of Jayalalitha Jayaram, the chief minister of Tamil Nadu, and the bride is the granddaughter of actor Shivaji Ganesan.

In addition to the challenge of learning to spell the names of their new in-laws, the families face a stack of wedding bills totaling $32 million. An intimate pre-wedding dinner was attended by 300,000 guests and was prepared by 3,500 cooks at a 30-acre estate covered with tents lit by chandeliers.

Two hundred truckloads of roses and jasmine carpeted a five-mile road for the bridegroom, who rode a sandalwood carriage drawn by six Arabian horses. Setting a new tradition of "something new, something blue, something borrowed, something noisy", hundreds of thousands of dollars' worth of fireworks were set off during the event.

So much for the idea of having a simple wedding. We can only hope the parents made the couple promise not to split up until the last wedding bill has been paid.

The mother of the bride shouldn't have had to worry about squeezing into a new dress. With that kind of money floating around, she could buy a new body.

Based on the size of a 30-acre estate and 300,000 guests, the wedding was eligible for a zip code of its own. Considering population, the wedding was larger than several other spots on the map, including Alaska, Iceland, Swaziland and Monaco. In fact, if the parents played their cards right, they could have applied for U.S. foreign aid based on the size of the wedding guest list.

The memories of the wedding would have lasted longer if, instead of covering five miles of road with 200 truckloads of flowers, the parents would have opted for taking the same amount of money and building a permanent expressway. As a personal touch, the paint lines could have been color coordinated with the bridesmaids' dresses.

The future social life of the newlyweds will be no problem. They may not be aware of it, but turnabout is fair play when it comes to invitations. For the next several decades they will be invited to countless thousands of weddings, baby showers and Tupperware parties.

Because 300,000 guests came to the wedding, the couple will spend the next 25 years writing thank-you notes. In fact they will still be thanking guests long after the warranties have expired on their 20,000 toasters and 30,000 microwave ovens.

Post-Natal Insurance Blues

How long should a mother stay in a hospital after giving birth? Some insurance companies seem to be leaning toward 30 minutes.

The hospital stay issue is one of the hottest debates between insurance companies, physicians, patient advocates and members of Congress. The bad news is that most of the members of Congress are men. The good news is that they're thinking of bumping up the minimum hospital stay from 12 hours to 48 hours. That's roughly the time it takes some people to commute to work during rush-hour traffic.

As a woman who has given birth and has the stretch marks to prove it, I believe this should be an issue largely determined by women. Having men make those decisions is tantamount to having women tell lube mechanics how long it should take to do their cars.

In both of these cases, the response would be, "I'll be done when I'm good and ready. What's it to you?"

After giving the matter considerable thought and trying to remember the life and times of the Dark Ages, when I actually gave birth, I have come up with the following guidelines, which should only be used in extreme cases. Early dismissals after 48 hours should only be granted if:

-The sex of the baby has been determined, toes have been counted and the baby has been given a name.

-The mother can walk without assistance and without clutching her abdomen with both hands.

-The mother and baby have had at least one meal.

-The delivery room has been readied for the next

patient.

Finally, no new mother should be dismissed from a hospital until she is capable of dressing herself without falling over.

An ideal situation would have new mothers staying in the hospital for longer lengths of time. Depending on the particular needs of the patient, this could vary from three days to ten years. With more lenient guidelines the mother and new baby wouldn't leave the hospital until:

-All of the birth announcements have been mailed out and thank-you notes have been written for baby gifts.

-The woman can walk out of the hospital in last year's blue jeans.

-Her friends and neighbors have been able to clean her house and fill her freezer with enough one-dish meals to sustain her family for up to one year.

-Doctors have been able to observe certain facts about her baby, including the first tooth and the baby's first attempts at walking.

In any case, once a woman learns she is expecting another child, she should lose all claims to post-natal recovery and she should be dismissed from the hospital accordingly.

My Introduction To Computers

The part of my brain that should understand modern technology isn't user-friendly. To be honest, I'm still recovering from the euphoria and excitement caused by transistor batteries and color television.

That intellectual deficiency became perfectly clear during recent encounters with a CD player and the Internet.

We were slow to buy a CD player. For all we knew, it would go the way of the Edsel or eight-track tapes. When it was finally purchased, we were pleasantly surprised to find the unit had two features with which we were vaguely familiar, a radio and a cassette player.

The CD component was more of a mystery. For the longest time, I've wondered why people would want to be entertained by certificates of deposit. If monetary matters become part of the entertainment industry, it won't be long before bank statements are used for leisure time reading.

"Insert disk on opened tray", read the directions, which were fairly easy to read once they had been translated from the original Japanese. When I saw what appeared to be a tiny turntable and the size of the 45 RPM record in my hand, I knew I had crossed a significant time warp.

The second encounter took place this week when I was hired to write an article for the Internet. For all I knew, Internet was the name of a fishing magazine.

When my contact for the article led me into his office, I knew how Dorothy must have felt when she landed in Oz. The room was alive with wall-to-wall computer thingamajigs. They beeped and buzzed and the monitor screens flashed with brilliant colors.

As he pulled an extra chair up to the largest machine, my contact turned and asked, "So, what computer do you write on at home — a 'excvbbn' or a 'nmkjlo?'" I'm quite sure those were his exact words. I instinctively knew he wouldn't be satisfied with a simple answer like "pen and paper".

"A word processor", I finally stammered.

From the open-mouthed look on his face, it was obvious he was thinking, "When it comes to the information highway, this woman has either pulled over at a rest stop or she has stalled out at the toll booth."

Finally, refusing to accept the fact I was a lost cause, he patiently explained the Internet. As I understand the system, it's a way for people with computers to talk to other people with computers about their computers. It's all very complicated.

When "Windows 95" sounds like an item on this year's housecleaning work list and "interfacing" reminds you of a ballroom dance step, you shouldn't fool around with computers.

By the end of our orientation session, a compromise was finally reached. I will type the article and turn it in and it will be placed on the Internet by any 15-year-old he chooses randomly from the street.

While my contact for the article had a vast menu to offer, I only wanted a little byte.

Ed And Bill Find The Cure For Acne

Before you replenish supplies in your medicine chest, you might consider two of the latest medical findings. If you happen to have a deer still tied to the top of your car or the ingredients for oatmeal cookies in your kitchen, a trip to the drug store might be unnecessary.

Researchers from Humboldt State University in California have reported that the toe jam of black-tailed deer contains chemical compounds that can kill several common types of bacteria (including one that causes acne) and fungi (including one that causes athlete's foot). The compounds are presently being duplicated by an Arizona pharmaceutical firm.

News of this type makes us wonder how the discovery was made in the first place. I would like to think the toe jam discovery was made by a couple of hunters, Ed and Bill.

(Camera pans the foothills of Wyoming. The final rays of the bright pink sun have almost completely disappeared and two hunters are spotted, huddled by the dying embers of their campfire. The darkened area around them is enveloped by an eerie silence, known only to a select group of men, willing to pay up to $2,000 for 40 pounds of venison.) Ed is the first to speak.

"You know, Bill, life doesn't get much better than this. We've both bagged our deer and we've got enough gas to get back to town. Only one thing bothers me, though. It's this embarrassing case of acne."

"Uh-huh. I've been giving your problem a great

deal of thought. Have you ever thought about scratching your face with one of those deer hooves hanging over the windshield of the car? That might help. Now that I think about it, why don't I join you? My feet are itching like crazy."

So it was that medical history was made.

Half a world away, in Japan, customers are lining up to buy the latest dieting product, Seaweed Defat Soap. Costing $15 a bar, the soap is believed to bubble away extra pounds. According to the Economist, the soap looks like lard imbedded with flecks of oatmeal.

At one point, someone in Japan had to stop eating an oatmeal cookie and instead rub the remainder onto his or her skin. With that action, a special treat became a topical preparation for weight loss.

It only seems natural that by spreading high calorie foods onto our skin, instead of eating them, we are bound to lose weight. If the fad catches on, people may soon be doing the same thing with chocolate candy bars, potato chips and slices of pizza.

Workers in fast food restaurants will soon be asking, "Is this order for take-out or will you be rubbing it on yourself here?"

Medical discoveries - they're not just for scientists anymore.

The Queen Of Clubs

My life is similar to a playing card — I have unwittingly become the queen of clubs. I should have known that purchasing clubs were becoming an obsession when their punch cards began taking over my billfold and I was seriously giving thought to throwing away my social security card and driver's license to make room for more.

The cards make me eligible for special bonuses when it comes to buying CDs and cassettes, cups of cappuccino, coffee beans, books, shoes and hosiery or renting movies. For example, if I buy six cups of mocha latte and have my card punched for each purchase, I'm entitled to a free seventh cup.

To paraphrase the late Duchess of Windsor, a woman can never be too thin, too rich or have enough espresso in her system.

My husband first became aware of my club memberships last week while we were doing some early Christmas shopping. As we stood by the hosiery counter in a large department store, the clerk routinely asked, "Are you a member of our hosiery club?"

"Oh, yes," I replied. My husband's obvious surprise was compounded when I fumbled with my billfold and punch cards from numerous clubs spewed all over the floor. As we rescued the scattered cards from the foot traffic around us, he asked, "What is a hosiery club? How often do you meet?"

As I tried to explain how by spending a small fortune on pantyhose I could get a free pair, his first reaction was that I was speaking a foreign language.

Spending money in order to save money seems to be too abstract an idea for some people. As his eyes glazed over with a "Don't tell me about it, I already know too much" look, I sensed my explanation was falling on deaf ears.

Judging from the look in his eyes, I knew he wasn't ready to hear about my more complex membership in the CD-cassette club. By reading the small print in the club contract, it's possible to receive as many as 12 CDs for ninety-nine cents. In addition, if I turn in the names of 20 close friends and their bank deposit numbers, I stand the possibility of adding 12,000 more CDs to our collection. By checking a secret box on the next order form and sending in 40 additional names, it's very possible that I could gain controlling stock in Columbia House.

Actually, my husband's comment about the clubs holding meetings might not be all that foolish. What better foundation for a hosiery club than foundation garments themselves? Discussion topics at meetings could range from "Pantyhose ankle droop" to "Nail polish for nylon repair - clear or coral pink?"

A hosiery club would also be the perfect setting for the expression heard most often at other, more traditional meetings - "Sorry, I gotta run."

Take-Out Dining

According to a survey by the American Restaurant Association, more than half of all restaurant dining experiences now involve take-out food. Leisure restaurant dining is quickly being replaced by burgers wrapped in paper and pizza eaten directly from cardboard boxes.

Changes are also being noticed in American homes. Children who once complained about their mothers' home cooking have been replaced by children who complain about the toys in their Happy Meals. A kid with a balanced diet has become a kid with a burger in one hand and a bag of french fries in the other.

If this trend continues, certain expressions will be dropped from our language — "making a meal from scratch" and "home cooking". Holiday meals will become things of the past because nobody will know how to prepare them. Instead of heading for grandmother's house and a meal featuring roasted turkey, mashed potatoes and gravy, families will sing, "Over the river and through the woods, to the fast food restaurant we go..."

Mothers will no longer be motivated to discuss favorite recipes during coffee breaks with their friends, but they will instead swap fast-food coupons.

This means that after another generation, people will be incapable of making lime gelatin salads with crushed pineapple and miniature marshmallows or hot dishes held together with cream of mushroom soup. It will mean the demise of authentic American cuisine.

Traffic mishaps will increase dramatically as drivers, mostly mothers and fathers, speed home with bags of take-out food, hoping to keep it warm.

Large kitchens will no longer be major selling points when homes are placed on the market. The houses commanding the highest prices will be those surrounded by the greatest number of take-out restaurants.

Companies manufacturing dishes, tablecloths, cookware and eating utensils will notice substantial declines in their sales as more and more people eat food with their hands, using the paper wrappers as placemats. Eventually we may forego the niceties of paper wrappers and simply eat with our hands while squatting on our haunches. We will become throwbacks to our earliest ancestors, who lived in caves and didn't have Martha Stewart books filled with tips for elegant dining.

Collectibles at future flea markets will include electric frying pans and, for that matter, any appliance or gadget related to food preparation.

Haute cuisine will no longer exist. The closest we will come to sophisticated dining will be when we insist upon "french fries du jour" and "hamburgers au jus."

However, some things will never change. Children and husbands will continue to ask, "What? This again?"

Exciting Drivers Training Update

Road & Track magazine reports that in nearly 1,000 high schools in 14 states, driver's education programs include instruction in using cellular phones while driving.

It's good to see a high school class adjusting to the times. When I took the course 41 years ago, driver's education teachers were operating under the theory that you shouldn't drive a car until you know how it works. Given that approach, we wouldn't be able to take antacids without understanding the complexities of the gastro-intestinal system.

I must admit that pistons and flywheels have never surfaced in a conversation since my graduation. Very few, if any, people go out for lunch and talk about internal combustion engines.

Teaching teens how to talk on a car phone while driving is only a start. If driver's education teachers wish to be practical they should also include the following topics in their lesson plans:

How to stay on the road when a toddler in the back seat covers your eyes with both of his hands and asks, "Guess who?"

How to apply makeup while driving to work. Why else would the driver have a make-up mirror?

How to balance french fries, a burger and a soft drink on your lap while driving.

How to remove the stains from those foods from the front seat upholstery.

How to get by in life without having to change a tire.

How to cover up those bothersome warning lights with duct tape when they insist on blinking. At the end of a busy day the last thing we need to see is some red light signalling,"Oil! Oil! Oil!"

How to reset the digital clock on the dashboard in rush hour traffic.

How to repair door dings with matching fingernail polish.

How to scrape dead bugs from the front of the car without removing the top two layers of paint.

How to transport an eight-foot Christmas tree on top of a six-foot car without obscuring your vision.

How to read an automobile insurance policy.

How to run eight errands in five minutes.

How to keep your driver's license picture from looking like the mugshot on a most-wanted poster.

How to keep a straight face when lying about your actual weight at the driver's license office.

Last but not least, a good driver's education course should teach us how to dress for an appearance in traffic court. That would be particularly useful information for people receiving phone calls and in-car faxes while they're driving.

Is It Chicken Or Pheasant?

The Iowa pheasant hunting season drew to a close this week. It ended with neither a bang nor a whimper. Instead, thousands of relieved wives across the state found themselves doing cartwheels.

To mark the occasion, countless wildlife cookbooks were relegated to back shelves of kitchen cupboards and guns were cleaned for one last time. I don't have anything against pheasant hunting. What bothers me most is figuring out new ways to disguise the bird's flavor before it reaches the dinner table.

During the past hunting season, I tried almost every recipe known to modern man as I attempted to make pheasant taste like chicken. That's not as easy as it may sound, although some women are capable of making venison taste like beef, frog legs taste like chicken and turtles taste like veal.

While the creative side of my brain sought out every imaginable culinary tactic — smothering the birds with cream of mushroom soup, burying them in fried onions or drowning them in white wine — the logical side of my brain kept asking, "Why?"

The creative side of my brain likes the idea of hunting. It likes the concept of living off the land and having a husband willing to kill for the sake of his family. Why else would grown men leave the warmth of their homes and tromp through unplatted marshes, stubbly cornfields and other wastelands in a frantic quest for a two-pound bird?

Although wives may favor blue-jeans and sweatshirts over the skins of wild animals worn by our foremothers, seeing a husband trudge to the door with a full day's beard and a bird in each hand is delightfully primeval. It may not be Kevin Costner at the door, but it does mean something to be married to a man who dances with pheasants.

Modern hunters may no longer drop their game birds on a cave floor and grunt, "Cook bird", but there is something wildly exciting about seeing a man, covered with cat-tail fluff, mud and snow, track across a newly cleaned kitchen floor.

The logical side of my brain keeps reminding me that what he paid for the hunting license, gun shells and other incidental costs — laundry detergent for his hunting clothes and hot water for his showers — amounts to a sum slightly less than the national debt. For the same amount of money we could buy a side of beef for the freezer and our family would be able to launch its own space program.

The creative side of my brain interrupts those thoughts. "Look at him," the creative side says. "You're married to a cross between Daniel Boone and Grizzly Adams. Life can't get much better."

"That's true, of course," argues the logical side, "if your idea of the good life is biting into stray buckshot when you're eating and having to make an emergency trip to the dentist's office."

While I may not like the taste of pheasant, I do love the hunter. I love him lock, stock and barrel and that's all that really matters.

Do-It-Yourself Coffins

Before you rush out and spend the money Aunt Maude included with your Christmas card or the refund you will surely receive from the Internal Revenue Service, you might consider one of the latest items on the market — a do-it-yourself coffin kit.

It's true. Apparently hoping to augment their farm income, a couple in River Falls, Wisconsin, Mary and Fred Lehmann, are sure consumers will soon be dying to buy their new product. The $989 kits contain hardware and precut wood of your choice. Overnight delivery is available.

The couple is also certain that the projects, if finished earlier than they're needed, might double as temporary bookcases or coffee tables.

That's all our household needs — another do-it-yourself project. It's one thing to live with unfinished sheet rock walls and plastic sheeting hanging from doorways during a lifetime of remodeling. It's quite another to navigate through a living room with an unassembled coffin as its conversation piece.

An unfinished coffin sitting in the middle of the floor would certainly cast a pall over most social gatherings.

"You have a great place here, Fred. Say, what's that you're building? A grandfather clock? A china cabinet for the missus?"

"Nope. It's a coffin."

Once the topic of the latest building project would be brought up, guests would leave without even trying the potato chips and onion dip. Coffins do that.

I also doubt whether the finished product would serve well as a temporary piece of furniture. Many people would feel uncomfortable putting their feet up on a coffee table engraved with the letters RIP. They may not appreciate the way cocktail napkins are tucked into the handles on the sides of the table.

On the other hand, having dual-purpose furniture — for instance, a coffin serving as a coffee table — would solve one dilemma in our home. After our daughters moved out and found places of their own, they found it cost efficient to furnish their new surroundings with valuables taken from our house during their visits.

By the time my husband and I turned 40, they figured we wouldn't need television sets, sheets, blankets or the microwave oven much longer. After we turned 50, our household furnishings had been fairly stripped down to the bare essentials. In return for our generosity, we were given numerous prom dresses, several dried-out corsages and a cardboard box filled with high school yearbooks.

"You want my china set? Go ahead, but the coffee table stays," they would be told.

The coffee table turned coffin would disprove one belief. You can take it with you.

We Become Politically Correct

Ordering check blanks by mail is almost as complicated as planning a meal for houseguests. Both activities have been affected by what's environmentally correct in the 1990s.

The ad for check blanks in the Sunday newspaper supplement noted that all of the company's designs "are printed on recycled check paper with 40 percent pre-consumer and 20 percent post-consumer waste." In addition, the check blanks are printed with biodegradable ink and a certain percentage of the sales will be donated to wildlife groups.

The business refers to itself as "an environmental check company." Ironically, the ad also mentions a $9.95 special on genuine leather checkbook covers.

It's all a matter of perception. Apparently, what's right for the trees in the Amazon and endangered species may not seem politically correct to a cow. The possibility of having one of her hind quarters turned into six or more checkbook covers might not seem like a good idea. She might be hesitant to turn the other cheek.

To further complicate matters, two lines in the ad read, "Check here if you do not wish to receive a vinyl checkbook cover. Help eliminate waste!" The oil well stays; the cow goes.

Preparing meals for houseguests has left me in a similar quandary. Only a few years ago, when a guest was asked, "What would you like for dinner?", the guest would demonstrate "midwestern nice" and say, "Don't go through any trouble. I'll have whatever you're having. Really, I don't want to be a bother. You've already gone out of your way by letting me use your bath towels."

Life was simpler then. Given the go ahead, hostesses could throw almost any dish on the dinner table. A heaping bowl of mashed potatoes, another bowl of lumpy gravy and a nice roast drowning in its own grease often brought rave reviews from guests at the table.

Now that guests travel greater distances and from towns with more than three stoplights and a cappuccino machine in every home, they have special requests at dinner time.

"Oops! I won't be able to eat that pork roast. I'm a vegetarian, but I do eat broiled chicken in emergencies."

"Sorry, but I'm lactose intolerant. Did you happen to put milk in those mashed potatoes?"

"I'll pass on the coffee. Do you have any cafe latte?"

"I should have told you before you made this meal, Grandma. I was just elected president of our school's animal rights group. I only eat eggs."

If this trend of turning ordinary hostesses into short order cooks continues, I fully expect a guest will someday tell me, "I'm sorry, but I don't eat food. I'll just have a glass of water and a vitamin pill."

Because I will want to appear environmentally and politically correct, I will just smile.

Luxury Hotel Suites

Before making your winter getaway plans, you might consider the new suites at the Hotel Inter-Continental in London.

While the hotel management says it is only trying to meet the growing demand for luxurious homes away from home, I'm sure of one thing. If our home was anything like their Royal Suite, I wouldn't be thinking about a getaway.

The suite includes a drawing room and library (the drawing room is large enough to park four Cadillacs), a dining room that can seat 10 and a fully equipped kitchen. There is also a music center with speakers in every room and a bed large enough to sleep 13 people comfortably.

Now for the bad news — the one-day rate for the Royal Suite is nearly $3,900.

Our family's idea of on-the-road lodging is quite different. In fact, you can be sure you're not staying at the Inter-Continental's Royal Suite when:

You find the fake oil paintings are bolted to the walls and the TV set is chained to the top of the dresser.

The complimentary bars of soap are so small that they only provide enough suds to wash two feet or one face and one arm. The choice is yours.

The bed spreads are of the scratch-and-sniff variety. Your head only has to turn slightly during the night to pick up a veritable smorgasbord of odors left by previous guests — greasy cheeseburgers, dogs with weak bladders and powder burns from Saturday night specials.

The fancy-sounding continental breakfast served in the motel entryway includes air-dried sweet rolls and coffee served in styrofoam cups. While you're deciding whether to try a roll, which promises to have the taste and texture of a hockey puck, a desk clerk named Flo or Rocky tells you more than you ever cared to know about hemorrhoid surgery.

You go outside to your car in the morning and find it's been stripped down to its wheel rims and someone has covered what's left of the car with crude, spray-painted messages, all somehow related to your mother.

The in-house movies on the TV include the latest Hollywood had to offer when the motel was built — "Gone with the Wind" and "Ma and Pa Kettle on the Farm".

The bathroom sink offers water with two temperatures — cold and very cold.

The walls are so thin that you think you know more about the couple staying in the next room than any other couple you've known before.

The registration form at the front desk requires you to list your next-of-kin.

The security chain inside your door has been sawed in half.

The only items on the room service menu are pork rinds and six-packs.

You have to look under the bed or behind a dresser to determine the original color of the carpeting in your room.

Perhaps the best indication that you're not staying in the Royal Suite is when you try to turn on the lights and discover the previous occupant stole all the light bulbs.

Chain Letter Anguish

Chain letters bear a striking resemblance to ransom letters sent out by kidnappers. Most often they are mailed in plain envelopes with no return addresses. The postmarks are usually smudged and hard to read. The addressee's name is in most cases hand-printed. What distinguishes the chain letter I received this week from all the others is that it doesn't ask that I send my favorite recipe to 10 other people. The recipe exchange chain letters operate under the theory that each participant should receive thousands of recipes in return.

This chain letter promises me luck and infinite wealth. By complying with the demands of the letter and sending 20 copies of the letter to my nearest and dearest friends, I will wallow in riches beyond my wildest dreams within four days. Failure to do so would mean spending the remainder of my life in abject poverty. The letter gives examples of people who gained vast amounts of money, ranging from $40,000 to over $7 million. The letter recipients who failed to follow the directions had relatives dropping off like flies and they lost whatever they had.

Actually, I was much better off before the letter arrived.

The letter was unsigned and the only name typed at the bottom of the page was that of St. Jude. You don't have to be a theologian to know that being called a saint implies that a person has been dead for a considerably long time. Either the letter had been sent under an assumed name or else it must have been a slow mail-day at the Vatican post office.

The only other possibility was that the letter had been re-routed through Chicago.

I had two problems with receiving the letter. First of all, what did the sender know about my life that I didn't know? I've been living a fairly charmed existence for the past few years. Why should I be forced to choose between good luck and bad luck and possibly upset the status quo?

The anonymous nature of the letter was also bothersome. What happens if, after mailing the letters, I receive the wrong luck? Suppose I get the 20,000 pounds of birdseed the woman with pet birds hoped to receive? What would I do with the newly restored engine for some guy's 1975 Ford Pinto? It may have been his fondest wish, but it wouldn't be high on my list of priorities.

The anonymity could be a curse rather than a blessing. I'm also reminded of what James Russell Lowell once said, "Granting our wish is one of fate's saddest jokes."

Time is running out and the letter is still sitting on my desk. I'm plagued by unanswered questions. Shall I invest $6.40 in postage stamps and immediately quit working? Do I have 20 friends?

Do I believe in luck? Deep down inside I believe there's no such thing as luck, but, just in case, it might be good to have it on my side.

A person can never really have too much birdseed.

Please Pass The Salicylates

The good news is that artificial flavorings in our food may be keeping us alive longer. Researchers from the National Center for Health Statistics in Hyattsville, MD, report that deaths from heart attacks have been on a sharp decline for the past 30 years. Because people in the 1960s were more interested in Ozzie and Harriet than healthy lifestyles, researchers have isolated what they believe is the true cause — artificial flavors based on salicylates, a chemical relative of aspirin. Those artificial flavorings are commonly found in baked goods, soda, candy, chewing gum, ketchup, ice cream, pudding, barbecue potato chips and even toothpaste.

One baby aspirin a day — a minor dose compared to the countless milligrams of salicylates consumed with our daily intake of junk food — is frequently recommended to ward off heart attacks, particularly in older people.

The bad news is that the word salicylates is difficult to pronounce. Future TV interviews with people who have turned 100 will underscore the difficulty. We've grown accustomed to hearing the interviewer ask the centenarian, "To what do you attribute your long life?" The answers have been fairly predictable — "I am fully dressed whenever I shower", "I only eat kiwi fruit" and my personal favorite, "I was never married."

It would be impossible to rattle off, "I owe my long life to salicylates", especially with a mouth which has been subjected to 100 years of dental work.

If artificial flavorings continue to affect our lives, they may also change one of the cliches most often heard in funeral homes. "My, doesn't he look natural?" would be replaced with "My, doesn't he look artificial?"

We should have noticed the significance of food additives in our lives long before the researchers did. Certain expressions began cropping up in our conversations: "She gave me one of her saccharin smiles" and "He looks well-preserved for his age."

In light of this news about artificial flavorings, it's also possible that researchers haven't considered the roles played by other food additives, such as food preservatives. If preservatives can give potato chips and Hostess Ho-Hos a shelf-life of at least 20 years, imagine what they can do for the people eating those foods.

Artificial food colorings may also have certain advantages. In that case, the correct response to having someone say, "Nice tan. Have you been south?", would be "Thanks, but what you see are food yellows #5 and #6."

The familiar phrases, "we are what we eat" and "living better through chemistry", take on new meanings with the addition of artificial flavorings, artificial colorings and preservatives to our diets.

In spite of the good news from the National Center for Health Statistics, it's still highly doubtful that our family doctors will tell us, "Eat a handful of barbecue potato chips and call me in the morning."

Weather Forecasters

Couch potatoes may finally have their day.

They no longer have to feel guilty about not leaving the house to buy pull-tabs or lottery tickets or driving long miles to gambling casinos. By simply sitting in their favorite chairs and staring at the television they may soon receive riches beyond their wildest dreams.

The latest get-rich-quick scheme involves suing TV weatherpersons. According to an article carried by the Associated Press, a woman in Haifa, Israel, is suing her local weatherman for $1,000 after he predicted sun for a day that turned out stormy.

She claims the weather forecast caused her to leave home lightly dressed. Because the forecast was inaccurate she caught the flu, missed four days' work, spent $38 on medication and suffered stress. In addition to the money, she also wants the weatherman's apology.

Weather forecasters are natural prey for lawsuits. They are probably the only workers who can be constantly wrong and still keep their jobs. One wag noted, "People who are afraid of being ruined by success should get a job with the weather bureau."

Of course, weatherpersons in our country prepared themselves for lawsuits long ago. That's when giving percentages became the meteorological equivalent of straddling the fence. Instead of predicting, "We'll have one inch of rain tomorrow", they began saying, "There's an 80 percent chance of precipitation tomorrow". Percentages give them win-win situations.

Other professions aren't allowed the same luxury when it comes to hedging answers. Imagine a doctor telling a patient, "You may or may not be healthy" or a car repairman saying, "Sure, I can fix your car. There's a 30 percent chance it will cost less than $250."

Judging from last month's weather, when days promised to be warm and sunny became close encounters with snow and sleet, weather forecasting appears to be as scientific as reading tea leaves or the bumps on a person's head. It's amazing that science can predict an eclipse of the sun many years in advance but can't accurately predict the weather for the next 24 hours.

Instead we are given 15 minutes of animated graphics and maps, signifying nothing. We are led to believe there's a difference between partly cloudy and partly sunny while they're the same thing.

If the lawsuits continue, we may soon hear cautious forecasters predict, "Tomorrow's going to be either hot or cold, and it may or may not rain." They may also follow the example set recently by a weatherman in a certain southern city when he announced, "For tonight, I predict darkness."

He undoubtedly had maps and charts to support his theory.

Why Midwesterners Never Sleep

When he was asked recently why manufacturing jobs in the rural portions of his state were on the rise, Minnesota Governor Arne Carlson had a quick answer.

"To many people in rural Minnesota, when they open up a plant at eight in the morning, they regard that as two extra hours of sleep."

Actually, he could have been describing the underlying work ethic in any rural area of the Upper Midwest, where sleep is considered a four-letter word. For all anyone knows, we don't engage in that particular activity.

Sleep is equated somehow with unproductive laziness and we go to great lengths to avoid words like "sleep" and "naps" in our vocabulary. At the end of a busy workday, as we collapse into our favorite chairs, we feel compelled to offer an apology by saying, "I think I'll rest my eyes" or "I'm just going to grab a little shut-eye".

What we do next may resemble sleep, but we prefer to call it dozing. In our minds, which have been trained since birth that "idle hands are the devil's workshop", catching some shut-eye in an upright position is much more acceptable than succumbing to a comfortable bed. We may be snoring during the prime-time television hours and we may be drooling on the pages of the TV Guide spread out on our laps, but we give the appearance that we could spring into action at any given moment.

It may look like sleep and sound like snoring, but we will deny ever doing those things.

If the phone should ring during the middle of the night, I'm conditioned to jump from the bed and stand at bleary-eyed attention.

"Did I wake you?" asks the caller.

"Oh, no," I protest. "I was just stripping floor wax in the kitchen." If I wish to inflict guilt upon the caller, I might add, "Never sleep, you know. There's so much to be done and little time to do it.""

I don't have the nerve to admit that only split-seconds before the call, I was sound asleep, dreaming about being stranded on a deserted island in the South Pacific with Robert Redford. I fail to mention that I was wearing a sarong similar to the ones worn by Dorothy Lamour in her movies and that answering the phone was the last item on my agenda.

An older friend of mine once confided that when she moved from Minneapolis to rural Minnesota as a young bride, she was shocked to see freshly laundered sheets hanging from her neighbors' clotheslines when the sun rose on Monday mornings. Wanting to sleep in on those days — yet not wishing to appear lazy — she would grab a pile of sheets from the linen closet on Sunday nights, immerse them in water and hang them on her clothesline. By creating the illusion that she never slept, she was welcomed with open arms into the community.

It's not that rural Midwesterners need less sleep than the rest of the world. They simply don't talk about it.

Thoughts Before The '96 Summer Olympics

People will be traveling great distances for two reasons this summer. One destination will be the Olympic Games held in Atlanta. The other will be the steady stream of out-of-town guests to the homes of people living in vacation areas. Actually, anyone living near a major highway runs the risk of having his or her home turned into a drop-in bed-and-breakfast this summer.

While the competitive events at Atlanta will involve running, jumping, swimming, lifting and throwing, private homes will offer non-traditional competitions such as marathon eating, sun-tanning and bath towel usage.

"Mankind is divisible into two great classes," noted the Reverend H.C. Beeching around the turn of the century, "hosts and guests."

Hosts living near lakes or theme parks would do well to follow the example set by Atlanta as they face swarms of visitors this summer. Before opening their doors to third cousins twice-removed from Keokuk or the aunt and uncle touring the country in their motor home with their four dogs and eight cats, prospective hosts should consider setting down a few rules. Atlanta did.

According to Fitness magazine, Olympic Game spectators won't be able to bring the following items to the events: knives, firearms, plastic toot horns, Frisbees, picnic baskets, ice chests, baby strollers, bottles, cans, pets, banners and full-sized national flags.

If they can set up those rules, why shouldn't private home owners have the same freedom? Before guests descend upon our lake home this summer, they would be wise to leave the following items at home: physical fitness magazines, aerobic exercise video tapes, house-cleaning tips, pets and requests for special diets. By their doing so, this world will be a much better place.

Fitness magazines make me feel guilty about letting my body go to seed. While other people's bodies may be seen as temples, mine is a two-bedroom rambler with an unattached garage. In addition, the magazines and workout tapes become little more than dust collectors after the guests have left.

Unless the visitors want to actually pitch in and help with the work, they should keep their house cleaning tips to themselves. While I'm balancing on a shaky stepladder washing second-story windows, and they're sunbathing on the deck below, the very last thing I need to hear is, "Have you ever tried shining those windows with crumpled newspapers?"

When it comes to pets, visitors should be advised that unless it is going to become the main entree for the next meal, any creature with four legs in our home is animala-non-grata. It's difficult enough to clean up the messes left by people.

Requests for special diets will simply fall on deaf ears. I've never fantasized about becoming a short order cook. On a rotating daily basis, the summer fare for visitors in our home includes grilled hamburgers and potato salad. On alternating days, guests are served potato salad with hamburgers. When I'm feeling particularly creative, paprika will be sprinkled with reckless abandon on the potato mixture.

In exchange for these considerations, guests in our home may expect to have their bed sheets changed at least once a month, to be given free access to an ample supply of freshly laundered bath towels and to have an endless supply of hot water for their frequent showers.

Being a guest or being a host requires making certain concessions. Maarten Maartens summed up the situation when he observed, "Staying with people consists in your not having your own way, and their not having theirs."

Let the games begin!

Coupon Mania

Have you become the coupon king or queen at your local grocery store? Do you find yourself living for the weekends, when the coupons are delivered in the Sunday newspaper? If these questions apply to your current lifestyle, you have come to the right place.

The following check-list will help determine if you have a problem with those cents-off coupons. Are you in control of the coupons, or are they in control of you?

You know you have a problem if you begin a coupon-clipping session when your children are still toddlers, and when you take your first break, they're graduating from high school.

Your youngest child is old enough to drive, but you find the disposable diaper coupons too good to ignore.

No longer content to redeem coupons for only things you normally use, you begin expanding your horizons. You don't have a pet, but you have several 50-pound bags of dog food stashed away in the garage.

You begin setting the alarm clock for four o'clock on Sunday mornings, allowing you plenty of time to rifle through the coupons in your neighbors' newspapers.

You save $5,000 by spending $25,000 — which also happens to be your annual income — at the grocery store. You have to sell your car and find a second job because you're saving so much money.

One closet in your house is filled to the ceiling with unopened packages of disposable razors, and another is filled with boxes of garlic-flavored (Try them! New and improved! Five cents off!) salad croutons.

Your hand is perpetually clenched in a scissors-cutting position.

For lack of any other interests in life, you name your children Bar Code, Expiration Date and Cents Off.

You become giddy and light-headed on "double coupon days".

You have nightmares about sleeping through a coupon expiration date.

Without thinking, you automatically tear coupons from magazines in the doctor's waiting room or in other people's homes.

It takes you four hours to buy groceries — 20 minutes for pushing the shopping cart through the store and the remainder of the time for sorting through mountain-high piles of coupons at the checkout counter.

While coming out of general anesthesia, you demand to know if the hospital accepts coupons. A dozen Franco-American Spaghetti coupons should surely cover a gall bladder surgery.

Remember this: a shopper with coupons should definitely exercise shelf-control.

South Dakota's Toe Service

The number of trees in South Dakota is exceeded considerably by its number of billboards. That was my observation after driving recently to Pierre to attend the state newspaper convention.
Amazingly, it wasn't a Wall Drug sign that was the most interesting. Drivers and car passengers become rather jaded after seeing countless signs proclaiming the virtues of that particular business: "Ice Water. Wall Drug. 351 Miles." or "Flush toilets. Wall Drug. 350 Miles."
The most intriguing series of signs was found near Mitchell and the massive billboards advertised a body shop run by a man named Dave, Bob or Jim. The name of the shopowner wasn't all that memorable, but I'll never forget the legend running across the bottom of the billboard: "24-Hour Toe Service".
Never before in my life had I heard of a car body shop dealing with actual human body parts. The word Toe wasn't offset by quotation marks, indicating that a great inside joke was going on between the casual passerby and Dave-Bob-Jim. The other words on the sign gave no hint of a great joke in progress.
The first possibility that entered my mind was that a successful podiatrist had once traveled that same interstate. After having his mind similarly numbed by the proliferation of billboards, he decided to abandon his lucrative practice and set up a second, perhaps more profitable, career. He would own a car body shop.
It's a well-known fact that people with smashed-up cars are often linked with a particular foot problem.

Most of us simply refer to this problem as "having a heavy foot" — a natural for a podiatrist with a second career.

Perhaps Dave-Bob-Jim set out to be a body shop owner in the first place. Unfortunately, his wife, a beautician specializing in pedicures, was unable to locate a position nearby. She is the person at the body shop with the 24-hour toe service.

Dave-Bob-Jim and his wife are quite happy with the combination business. While he pounds out fenders and prepares cars for their new coats of paint, his wife, Linda, Betty or Wanda, covers the customers' toes with a matching color. Linda-Betty-Wanda's professional favorites are Collision Coarse Red, Fender Bender Fuschia and Door Ding Pink.

A third possibility is that Dave-Bob-Jim has a particular quirk to his personality - in this case, a toe fetish. At any hour, day or night, he will drive his shop truck great distances to catch a glimpse of a toe. It could be worse. He could have a foot fetish, which would qualify him for a guest seat on almost any daytime talk show.

The only other scenario is too disturbing to think about. Dave-Bob-Jim and the sign maker can't spell.

My Sweepstakes Friends

I don't write personal letters very often. As a result, my only correspondence lately has been with people I've never met — namely Anne, Pauline and Elizabeth.

Although each woman has her own distinct personality, they all have two things in common — they all run national sweepstakes contests and they all want to see me win.

Pauline and I have had the closest relationship. She works for a large flower bulb company in Michigan, and almost daily she sends me another letter, requesting that I punch out certain stamps affixed to the letter and apply them to my contest entry form and the return envelope.

Because of Pauline my scissors-cutting and licking skills have improved considerably. The change is so great that my right hand is developing small calluses and my tongue is often stuck to the roof of my mouth.

Pauline has a strong work ethic. She believes people should work for any money they receive. She could have sent me my $250,000 months ago, but she won't feel satisfied until I've followed her instructions to the letter.

Anne never wanted to be a sweepstakes manager for Reader's Digest. She wanted to be a novelist, dealing with cloak-and-dagger espionage and people wearing trenchcoats. This fact became obvious yesterday when I received the following notice from her:

"At exactly 8:30 a.m., on the morning of September 20, a bonded security agent, dispatched from the treasurer's office of W.H. Magill, will board a jet at White

Plains Executive Airport in Westchester County, New York. Handcuffed to the agent's wrist will be a locked, metal briefcase containing $23,500 in cash and a confidential 9-digit code number.

"If the number in the agent's briefcase matches the one on the attached card, he'll be on his way to O'Hare International Airport and your home in Spirit Lake."

Anne hasn't stopped to consider that O'Hare is 600 miles from where I live. While caught up in plot development, she hasn't thought about my feelings about drop-in company. Will I be expected to serve the agent coffee and something to eat? Where will the agent sleep?

Elizabeth, on the other hand, tends to be more mean-spirited in her role as sweepstakes director for a large book clearing house. In her latest letter, she described how a guy named Robert Riddle and I have been confirmed as $1 million winners. She quickly added, "Unlike Robert Riddle, you won't lose a penny of your $1 million to taxes. We'll pay you a $666,675 tax bonus."

I can only wonder why Robert Riddle is being treated so unfairly. Does Elizabeth feel this way about all men named Robert? Did a guy named Robert fail to show up for her high school prom?

I'll wait until she's ready to talk about it.

My New Age Sister

I have a very up-to-date sister. She's only six years younger than I am, but at times we seem eons apart in our interests.

While she was visiting me recently, we were both invited to what the hostess called "a women's meeting". Aromatherapy would be involved in the evening's activities. Something was also said about communing with a nearby lake, whatever that meant.

This New Age business, although it's been around since the 1980s, is all very new to me. Until my sister's visit, New Age was telling someone an age other than the one listed on my driver's license.

"We would love to come," my sister told the hostess, only seconds before I could give my standard excuse about having to wash my hair. She and the hostess began talking about my sister's Tai Chi classes, and I knew instantly I was out of my league.

For one thing, my untrained ear led me to believe that my sister was talking about "Thai cheese classes". Although I was only familiar with cheddar, edam, gouda and parmesan cheeses, I figured that any activity having to do with food couldn't be all that bad.

It wasn't surprising that my sister knew something about foreign cheeses that I didn't. She has also experienced sweat lodges in Northern Michigan, healthy foods, meditation and running for the sake of running.

On the other hand, I spend most of my time wondering if there will ever be fat-free Twinkies, if my body will eventually adjust to the side-effects of olestra and if manufacturers will continue to produce clothing with elastic waistbands. I tend to back off when people talk about getting in touch with their innermost feelings.

I began having second thoughts about an hour before the meeting was scheduled to begin. Would this be a touchy-feely encounter session? How does a person talk with a lake? Would I be able to keep my clothing on? Would I be beaten with willow branches? I abhor pain.

"Don't worry," my sister reassured me. "I'll make some healthy food for us to take along. Wear some gemstones and, please, try to avoid wearing synthetic fabrics."

Armed only with a black bean chip dip, heavily laden with fresh herbs, we left the house.

The session went pretty well, considering that my last all-women meeting had been in 1974 when I was forced into attending a Tupperware party. Before our small group walked along the lakeshore and watched a spectacular sunset, we sprayed our faces and inhaled fine mists made from heather and mint oils. Although I had taken a vow of silence before my sister and I left the house, everyone thought I became particularly chatty after the mint oil episode.

It was an evening well spent. Heather oil, anyone?

Lost In Rural Space

"Are you lost daddy I asked tenderly.
Shut up he explained."
Ring Lardner, The Young Immigrants.
1920.

Like the family described by Lardner 76 years ago, thousands of vacationers are venturing into unknown territories this summer. They travel where street addresses don't exist and where directions seem to be given in a language different than their own.

They aren't lost in the Australian outback or some other foreign country. They are losing their bearings in rural America.

Everyday I watch them drive back and forth on the gravel road in front of our house, searching aimlessly for their destinations and clutching tightly to crumpled maps which make no sense. The seemingly endless parade includes motor homes, cars towing boat trailers and scores of family mini-vans with kids asking the drivers, "Are you lost, daddy?"

Most of the travelers were in trouble long before they packed their vehicles and backed out of their driveways. They shared the mistaken belief that all people and vacation resorts in this country should be easy to find. For that same reason, I often prepare meals for guests who show up two, three or even four hours late.

Rather than having house numbers and street signs, we only have winding miles of unmarked township and county roads. In fact, the gravel road running past our house is represented by a thin dotted line on most maps and is often misinterpreted as a crease in the paper.

One night last week, as I prepared dinner for a guest driving down from Minneapolis, the phone rang. She was calling from her car's cellular phone and she needed last minute instructions for the final miles of her trip into the hinterland.

"I was fine until I left the interstate," she told me, but I can't make sense out of your directions."

"Don't worry," I reassured her, " you're only 15 miles away. Go south for eight miles, then west for seven miles to where the Loon Lake Store used to be, then three-fourths of a mile until you hit the first gravel road going south. Ours is the first house past the trailer park. You can't miss it."

My instructions fell on deaf ears. For all she knew, I was reciting ancient Arabic poetry.

"What is this — a geography class? I don't know south or north. I only know left and right. How many minutes are you away?" She hung up the phone before I could give her a complete translation.

One hour and one shriveled up roast beef later, she called again and she sounded desperate.

"I don't know where I am. I'm surrounded by green fields and everything looks the same. I can drive through New York City, but I can't find your house. My high school class chose me as the likely to succeed. Maybe I should turn around and just go home."

Our cultures had clashed head-on. Understanding directions in a rural area requires knowing what family occupied a certain house 40 years ago ("Turn north at the Johnson place") or obscure events in history

("Turn south at the corner where Olson's brakes went out on his '50 Ford").

Four phone calls and two hours later, our guest finally reached our doorstep with a clump of wilted flowers clenched in her hand. The roast beef resembled a large charcoal briquet, so we heated up a frozen pizza instead. We always keep an ample supply of pizzas in the freezer for out-of-town dinner guests. They seem to prefer them.

Convenience Stores

While doing some casual research for this week's topic — gas stations — I found a quote by someone named Marchant. I have no idea who this Marchant person was. For all I know, he or she was a entertainment celebrity, following the one-name gimmick used by Prince, Madonna and Liberace.

Marchant noted, "To be a success in business, be daring, be first, be different." If he was an early Roman, he could have been talking about the up-and-coming chariot trade. If he lived during this century, he was undoubtedly referring to the gas station business.

Gas stations, formerly called service stations, are taking on a new name these days — convenience stores. Most places selling gas no longer have employees willing or able to look under the hood, to wipe the oil dipstick on their overalls as they check the oil level, or to scrape flattened bugs from windshields. Of course, those activities date back to the days when you could buy four gallons of gas for a dollar, receive double trading stamps on Tuesdays and add another free drinking glass to your collection back home.

Gas stations are no longer what they appear to be as they diversify into other areas. As they struggle to be seen as daring, first and different, they now offer fresh-baked pizzas, groceries and a wide variety of services, including dry cleaning and photo developing. Few of the services are related to cars.

Diversification took a new direction last summer when a local convenience store posted a sign, "Cappuccino — Nightcrawlers". While traveling in northern Minnesota this week, I spotted one gas station called "Tank and Tackle" and another named "Bait and Bullets".

If this trend continues, we should expect other interesting combinations of gas products and services to appear along our streets and highways.

One combination could combine gasoline sales and psychological services for stressed out travelers — "Pavlov and Petroleum".

"Chips and Clips" could be the name of a convenience store specializing in snack foods and haircuts.

A store offering pet neutering services by a qualified veterinarian could be called "Free Air and No Heirs".

A car mechanic and a professional photographer could merge their skills and become "Camshafts and Cameras".

An artist, a florist, a chef and a mechanic could form "Pastels, Petals, Pasta and Pistons".

Somewhere down the road, pun intended, we might even find a gas business offering oil checks, clean windshields, free drinking glasses and double trading stamps on Tuesdays. With its shelves only displaying road maps, stale candy bars and a large container of beef jerky, it could be called a service station. That would truly be daring and different.

All You Need To Know About Golf

Joe Laurie, Jr. once observed, "Magellan went around the world in 1521 - which isn't too many strokes when you consider the distance."

His comment would have been even more humorous if I hadn't taken roughly the same number of strokes during my last golf game. Although words such as "par" and "birdie" are still not part of my everyday vocabulary, I don't believe my time on golf courses has been completely wasted. Like most activities in life, golf can be a learning experience. Here are a few of the lessons I learned this summer:

Never believe a golfer who says, "It's just a game." That person would also tend to minimize world wars, flu epidemics and stock market crashes.

Be prepared to lose when your opponent announces, "I don't care if I win or lose." There is also a strong indication that the player in question would lie about other things.

Never golf with a person nicknamed Babe, Ace, Bear or Ringer.

Although geometry teachers are quick to point out that the shortest distance between two points is a straight line, they should add, "Except on a golf green."

The flag on the next hole is always farther away than it appears to be.

Never expect a male foursome to allow two female golfers to "play through."

A "sand wedge" isn't something to eat.

It's possible to walk eight miles while playing a 300-yard fairway.

You won't be accepted as a serious golfer if you use pink golf balls or club covers resembling Walt Disney characters.

If someone inquires about your golf handicap, it's considered bad form to answer, "My partner."

Never — I repeat — never pick up lost golf balls while they're still moving on the ground.

Except in extreme cases, a golf ball lying eight feet from the cup should not be considered a "gimme".

If someone offers to play a friendly game for money, "friendly" isn't the operative word.

With enough practice, a "whiff" can resemble a practice swing.

No matter what your opponent says, a person can never have too many golf trophies.

Finally, Bob Hope knew what he was talking about when he noted, "If you watch a game, it's fun. If you play it, it's recreation. If you work at it, it's golf."

Although my golf scores don't show it, I've definitely been working.

Parenthood – A Moving Experience

One of our daughters, single and in her late 20s, recently had all of her worldly possessions moved from northern Minnesota to Rhode Island.

The mover she chose was highly recommended. He had already moved our daughters' belongings to and from college campuses and jobs in distant states a dozen times. And, yes, he would be willing to transport her goods and tow her car through 10 states in 33 hours. Above all, the move would be relatively inexpensive.

After our daughter had unpacked her things, she was dismayed to find one item missing. Like any conscientious consumer, she called the mover.

"One of my phones is missing," she lamented over the phone.

"Buy yourself another one," answered her father.

If parents who rent trucks to move their grown children from one place to another would be awarded frequent-mover miles, similar to the plan offered by airlines, my husband would be able to drive a Ryder truck around the world.

Archimedes, the Greek mathematician, once noted, "Give me somewhere to stand, and I will move the earth." Until we became parents and found ourselves in the moving business, we never realized that Archimedes also had children.

We are not alone. A friend told me this week that her husband was moving one of their daughters' things from Southern California to Sioux City. Another friend is also on the road, moving his daughter from Minnesota to Michigan.

Exact numbers aren't available, but at this very moment, countless, bleary-eyed parents are criss-crossing highways all over this great country with rental trucks and trailers, moving their offspring from Point A to Point B.

They exist on cold french fries from fast-food restaurants and they stare blankly at the road ahead as they sip lukewarm coffee from styrofoam cups.

As their children leave for college and jobs in distant cities, the parents find themselves loading their old, discarded furniture they had never hoped to see again. At their final destinations they lug large, cumbersome boxes up seemingly endless stairways and they somehow find the strength to build sleeping lofts in dormitory rooms slightly larger than postage stamps.

As they carry, bend, lift, hoist, stretch and climb, parents are using muscles they had forgotten existed. They are known at truck-rental places on a first name basis.

At a time when children are becoming more independent and moving farther away from home, they have at the same time become more dependent upon their parents to get them where they're going. I seriously doubt whether we have the physical strength to see our children become more independent.

Being a parent is definitely a moving experience.

The Magnificent Tomato Obsession

Former President George Bush would have referred to it as "the tomato thing." Whatever it's called, my craving for the taste of garden-fresh tomatoes traditionally peaks during the early months of summer. This year was no exception.

As soon as the final patches of snow had been shoveled from our garden plot and the remaining frost in the ground had been eliminated with the help of a hair dryer and a long extension cord, I planted 36 tomato plants. I hesitate to admit how many times those original plants were replaced in the wakes of recurring ice storms and snowfalls, but I was a woman possessed.

By the time warm weather actually rolled around, I was fantasizing on a regular basis about bacon-lettuce-and-tomato sandwiches. Each sighting of a new, yellow tomato blossom was accompanied by renewed hope and anticipation. The weeks passed by slowly and I could imagine biting into the first red tomato and experiencing the joy of having its excess juice and seeds roll down my chin.

The first tomato was everything I had hoped it would be. After plucking the first fruit of the season from its stem and holding it high in the air, I struck a pose similar to that of Scarlett O'Hara when she found the carrot in Tara's abandoned garden halfway through "Gone With the Wind."

That wasn't the only similarity. As the uplifted tomato soaked up the warmth of the midsummer sun, I found myself quoting her lines and shouting, "With God as my witness, I'll never be hungry again!" For as long as I can remember, I have always had a dramatic streak.

It wasn't as if there weren't enough potato chips and assorted party dips in the house to sustain our family for months, but holding the first tomato of the season was a special moment. The first tomato — sweet and succulent — was devoured as I stood in the garden.

Within a few weeks, the tomato dreams became nightmares. At first the novelty of having fresh tomatoes had me adding them with reckless abandon to every recipe in the house — stews, pasta dishes, scrambled eggs and everything else with the exception of pancakes. They were sliced, diced, fried, stewed, simmered and preserved. Tomatoes became my main preoccupation.

My life was clearly divided into two parts — before the tomatoes and after the tomatoes. Now that every window sill in the house has been completely lined with tomatoes, the refrigerator has been filled to capacity and every canning jar has been filled, the end still isn't in sight.

Unable to keep up with the proliferation of tomatoes, I am now foisting them upon unsuspecting strangers who show up at our door. A simple question — "Do you like tomatoes?" — may lead to the possibility of being buried in an avalanche of the things. The UPS man has made it quite clear that he doesn't require bushels of tomatoes in exchange for his package deliveries.

It is possible to have too much of a good thing. In a complete turnabout, my fantasies these days are about tomato blight and an early frost.

Mummifying Mom

Mummy's the word. Corky Ra, owner of a mummifying business called Summum Inc., has been perfecting his preservation method on more than 2,000 roadkill animals and on 30 cadavers purchased from a medical school.

His Salt Lake City company now has a waiting list of 137 humans, who promise to pay up to $30,000 for the process. The extra option of being converted into a bronze statue could cost as much as $100,000. The desire to become a Boris Karloff look-alike has its price.

The problems associated with becoming a statue are obvious. It's not as though a pair of baby shoes, destined to collect dust in the attic someday, are being bronzed. When survivors shell out so much money to have a dearly departed one bronzed, they will certainly want to show off their latest investment.

If one of Corky Ra's statue customers chooses a pose similar to that of the Statue of Liberty, he or she could double as a hat rack or a novelty cookbook holder in someone's kitchen. After crouching down on all fours and supporting sheets of glass on their backs, they could become coffee tables.

In that case, normally quiet people could become conversation pieces if they opt to become statues in their second lives. They will become the focus of attention in social settings and it will become common to hear comments such as, "Put the chip dip on Aunt Rosie, will you?" or "How many times have I told you to keep your feet off great-uncle George?"

There's also the possibility that a person could be transformed into a piece of outdoor sculpture. The prospect of becoming a pit stop for pigeons is considerably less glamorous than becoming a coffee table, and the statue would run the risk of having its feet shortened over the years with lawn trimmers.

A bronze statue could also face the same fate as old photos in a family album, which are eventually surrounded by anonymity. Over the years, names and faces slip from people's memories.

"What's that?" a descendant's friend would ask in the year 2089, tapping the statue's shoulder with a yet-to-be- invented lazer phazer.

"We have no idea", the statue's distant offspring would answer. "It's been around for years. To tell you the truth, we had hoped to get the family china."

My main objection to being mummified and becoming a bronzed statue is quite simple. After living an entire life without a single person telling me I look well-preserved, why should things change after I'm gone?

Our Guest, The Computer

Euripides observed, "Every man is like the company he is wont to keep." If that's the case, I played hostess for a dozen brunch guests and two computers last weekend.

Actually, the latter consisted of one man and his laptop computer. While the other guests contented themselves with muffins, a fruit medley and usual pleasantries, this particular male guest had what Julius Caesar referred to as "a lean and hungry look."

As it turned out, his hunger wasn't centered on muffins, eggs or fruit. After the dishes had been cleared away, he held up his laptop computer for everyone to see and asked, "May I tap into one of your phone lines?"

It was the first time a guest had asked to be linked up to our utilities. If he would have asked to tap into our furnace or water heater, his request would have sounded equally strange. Within the space of time it takes to say "worldwide web", he had the computer attached to our bedroom phone.

While the rest of the guests were engaged in lively conversation in our living room, he was in a world by himself. It wasn't as if he had vanished completely. From time to time, he would peek into the living room and share information from his laptop screen.

At one point, while most of us were discussing the upcoming presidential election, he interrupted, "Would anyone like a listing of Melissa Etheridge's concert dates for this year?"

Questions like that have a tendency to slow down

the flow of normal conversation.

"Not really," we murmured and he left the room. Later in the morning, as the guests in the living room exchanged photos of their vacations and grandchildren, he reappeared in the doorway.

"Would anyone like to surf with me?" he asked. It was an odd invitation, considering we live on dry land, thousands of miles from the nearest ocean.

"We could surf websites," he explained. When he could see there were no takers, he shrugged his shoulders and left the room.

Although I had heard about people who are addicted to conversations in cyberspace, I never expected to see a computer casualty in our own home. For all I knew, while the rest of us were chatting in the living room, our elusive guest was proposing marriage to a mother of eight children in Nashville. On the more positive side, he might have been learning about the average annual rainfall in Brazilian jungles.

When it came time for our guests to leave, the man's wife pried his fingers from the computer keyboard and unplugged the connection with his world. I'm almost positive I saw tears well up in his eyes when the computer screen went blank.

As we said our final goodbyes at the door, I told the man, "Thanks for coming. It was great seeing you again."

"Signing off," he mumbled.

Frank Lloyd Wright once described television as "chewing gum for the eyes". I wonder what he would have said about personal computers.

Hunger Awareness Month

When it comes to weight watching, October is the cruelest month of all. October has been set aside to celebrate the various products promoted by the American food industry.

For that reason, October is at the same time Seafood Month, Popcorn Month, Pizza Month and Pork Month. In an attempt to remind us that we always have room for one more slice of pizza, October has also been designated as Hunger Awareness Month.

Because each of these foods has been given holiday status, it would seem unpatriotic to ignore them. It would also be unpatriotic to ignore the holiday set aside for sugar and fat consumption, Halloween.

Through no fault of my own — the local stores began displaying Halloween candy in July — I have made at least 20 trips to town to replenish my supply of trick-or-treat candy. Realizing that some children like to get an early start at trick-or-treating, I began setting the candy basket by the front door on Sunday, October 6.

In light of the fact that I seldom use the front door, it seemed like a harmless plan. Even if I chose to grab a candy bar on the rare occasions I used the door, how could this holiday-preparedness plan possibly go wrong?

Within three hours after the plan and the candy basket were in place, the grand scheme for holiday treating began falling apart. The front door, the basket of candy next to it and I became inseparable.

For starters, the maple trees in the front hard had to be checked at least a dozen times that morning to see how much they grown during the summer. That same number of candy bars disappeared.

Another six bars were consumed when I poked my head out the front door to determine if the doorbell was in proper working order.

At least five more candy bars vanished into thin air when I made repeated trips to our roadside mailbox to confirm the fact that the U.S. Post Office doesn't deliver mail on Sundays.

The greatest flaw in my plan to treat every Halloween visitor at our door was based on self-deception. We haven't had a trick-or-treater at our house for as long as we've lived here. Most of the houses on our lake belong to summer residents and the places stand empty at this time of year.

However, optimism prevails. Every Halloween we turn on the front door light, sit by the door for several hours and wait for the doorbell to ring. As we wait, we sample the candy bars, testing their current levels of freshness.

Even though no trick-or-treater in recorded history has ever ventured down our isolated gravel road, we sit, unwrap candy bars, eat them and wait. During the course of the evening, the basket is constantly refilled with fresh supplies — just in case.

Halloween is clearly an appropriate way to end a month dedicated to seafood, popcorn, pizza, pork and hunger awareness.

The Body-Mass Index Is Explained

The scales have been tipped. For the first time in U.S. history, overweight people have become a majority, and folks at the National Center for Health Statistics are blaming our BMIs — our body-mass indexes.

Possible reasons given by the center for the dramatic increase are varied. They range from eating too much and exercising less to using the remote control for the TV. Coincidentally, the increase occurred at the same time the center began using the BMI.

Determining one's personal BMI is a complicated matter. It requires a calculator, the mental prowess of a rocket scientist and giving up several minutes of good eating time. I actually lost five pounds while trying to decipher my BMI.

The first step in determining a BMI involves multiplying your weight in pounds by .45 to get kilograms. Unless you're a world traveler used to the metric system, this is much easier said than done.

Personally, I don't trust our bathroom scale. Because its batteries are usually weak, the bathroom floor has an uneven surface and a multitude of other reasons, it tends to exaggerate true weights. The bathroom scale doesn't allow for the facts that my clothes are unusually heavy (about 50 pounds) and that my hair and fingernails should be trimmed (20 pounds). For the sake of demonstration, I am using 120 pounds or 54 kilograms, my actual weight in seventh grade.

The second step requires that we set this number aside while we do some other math. It is set aside in much the same way we set aside a pan of fudge to allow it to harden or the way a bowl of frosting is set aside because the cake is still in the oven. As a matter of fact, I am presently doing both of those activities.

Next, we must convert our height to inches. Although my driver's license lists my height at 68 inches, I prefer to use 69 inches. My posture leaves much to be desired.

The next step is tricky. We must multiply the inches by .0254 to get meters. Without a computer, this step is virtually impossible. Having done this, I found my height in meters to be 1.7526 and, for the sake of simplicity, I rounded the number up to two meters.

The fourth step requires us to multiply the number of meters by itself. This is as easy as pie. A piece of cake. Two times two is four.

In the final step of the BMI formula, this last number is divided into the number of kilograms, which had previously been set aside with the fudge and frosting. The resulting number, 13.5, is my BMI.

The center has determined that the normal range for weight is in the 20s and overweight isn't a factor until 30 is reached. I don't know about you, but I feel much better. Fudge with frosting, anyone?

Cleaning The Refrigerator

It may be too late by the time you read this, but November 20 is National Clean Out Your Refrigerator Day.

Some tasks are easier said than done. In extreme cases, cleaning out a refrigerator requires a gas mask, a strong stomach and the ability to deal with mutant life forms. The process is also time consuming.

Cleaning the refrigerator is one of the few chores which hasn't been made easier over the years. Before the event of frost-free refrigerators, cleaning the appliance was traditionally done on a monthly basis.

Armed with a boiling pan of water, a sturdy floor fan and a crowbar strong enough to chip away a foot of permafrost, earlier homemakers could accomplish their task in less than two days. They didn't have to worry about leftovers that were no longer recognizable or that were developing into intelligent life forms.

Ostensibly, setting aside a special day for refrigerator cleaning is a public health issue. Before we store leftovers from Thanksgiving this year we should do something about the pan of lasagna which has been tucked away in one corner of the appliance since 1986. It's time to deal with the furry potato salad your guests were unable to finish last July.

When I opened the refrigerator door this month and took a long, hard look at its contents, I was almost certain I could see alien life forms scampering for cover in the far recesses of the shelves. Listening to a hushed silence when you open a refrigerator door is not a good sign.

"What a mess!" I groaned.

"It's not that bad", answered the former head of lettuce.

"What does she want?" blubbered the blob of red, wrapped in plastic and soaking in its own juice. I vaguely recalled seeing a red bell pepper sitting in that same place three summers ago. In this case, time hadn't been kind.

"Pipe down, will you?" A plastic container trembled in the far reaches of an upper shelf. "I'm trying to study! Let's see - que' autobus pasa por aqui?" Leftovers from a memorable enchilada dinner in 1969 had spoken.

"What's happening?" screamed a frightened cluster of fuzzy grapes.

Beyond the clutter of nondescript leftovers and eggs and cheese chunks older than any of our children, other voices were soon raised in protest. The bright refrigerator light had interrupted their normally darkened lives.

I closed the door on the now deafening roar and the kitchen was quiet once more. Rather than clean out the refrigerator and destroy an entire subculture, I will instead observe Replace Your Full Refrigerator Week.

A Giant Jump For Mankind

Even when he was president, Harry S. Truman worried about his mother, his sister and their car. In a 1945 letter to them from the White House, he advised, "Keep 35 pounds of air in the tires and have it greased once in a while and have the oil changed every thousand miles."

It was sound, basic advice. Not surprisingly, he never mentioned what to do about a dead battery. As with many people, my brain will compute "grease job and oil change" but it short-circuits whenever someone refers to a car's vital organs. The part of my brain dedicated to knowledge of car engines, lawn mowers and other mechanical know-how has never been activated.

Instead, those mechanical facts are automatically regarded as useless and they are relegated to a junk drawer in my mind, never to be located again. In their cob-webbed surroundings, they join the method for finding the square roots of numbers, the exact date of the Boston Tea Party and the year Calvin Coolidge was elected President.

Certain lessons in life are forgettable. I wouldn't be able to tell a flywheel from a piston, although I'm sure the driver education teacher who first told me about those things thought they were pretty important. When I was 15, he literally wasted two hours of his life explaining how to change a tire. Coincidentally, that was the same year he decided to go into another field of work.

In his final words to me, he predicted that I would

spend the rest of my life like the Vivien Leigh character in "A Streetcar Named Desire". When it came to cars, I would always depend upon the kindnesses of strangers.

There were no strangers to help when my car battery died this week. Instead, I had to place at least four or five long-distance phone calls to my husband at his office for a crash course in battery starting.

After the first phone call, I was able to figure out how to open the hood of the car and I knew what a battery charger looked like.

The second phone call was filled with ominous warnings about how the car and I could be blasted into smithereens if the charger clamps would touch each other while the machine was turned on, if the clamps would be attached to the wrong thingamajigs on the battery or if I placed the charger on the car's fan blades. I was clearly entering dangerous ground.

As my brain chided, "This does not compute! Do not store for future use!", our fourth call was devoted to more than I cared to know about positive and negative terminals and wires coded with special colors.

Quite miraculously, the engine and I experienced a surge of power at the same time. The battery got the juice or whatever my husband said it needed, and I was ecstatic about my mechanical prowess. I am woman. My car roars.

The Complications Of Retirement

In eight short months, a man will be standing at my front door with a check in his hand. If everything goes according to plan, the check — my passport to fortune and riches beyond my wildest dreams — will be delivered by the postman, not Ed McMahon.

It will be my first teacher retirement check, and it will be sealed, signed and delivered by a state teacher retirement group in St. Paul. They're nice, helpful people and a few staff members know me by my first name. During my frequent calls to confirm that my mailing address is still the same and to remind them that I am ready, willing and able to receive that first check, they remain courteous and professional. I think they sense my excitement.

I placed one of those calls last Monday and told them I was ready to start signing the necessary forms for retirement. After noting my name and mailing address for one last time, the retirement advisor asked for my husband's name and address.

"Why would you want his name and address?" I asked him. "He's not retiring from teaching. I am."

"It's called spousal notification," explained the advisor. "According to state law, he must be told of your decision to retire."

"But can't you see that this is going to botch up my plans?" I joked. "I wasn't going to tell my husband. I was going to pretend that I was going to work and instead spend aimless hours shopping in malls and hanging out at libraries."

He laughed at my suggestion. A few days later,

when I decided to call someone else at the advisor's office and find out if what he said was true, the state law was explained in greater detail. Evidently, too many widows in the state were finding out too late that their spouses had left them without survivor benefits in their retirement plans.

I can accept a state law, but what I can't accept was what happened with my husband on that same Monday. In anticipation of an upcoming deer hunting trip, he purchased a 7-mm rifle with a 3X9 variable power scope, whatever that means.

I can't be sure, but from the way my husband described his new lethal weapon, he would be able to stand in Wisconsin and still do a fair amount of damage to the Statue of Liberty. With the scope's powerful capacity, he would be able to bag a deer in Wyoming without leaving our driveway.

"Did you have to fill out any forms when you bought the gun?" I asked him.

"Sure," he replied. "There were a few forms and I had to show the salesclerk a photo ID." No, he hadn't been told about any spousal notification.

State and county workers retiring in Minnesota are receiving mixed signals from the state legislature. We can't retire without spousal notification, but it's all right for our spouses to turn our homes into potentially dangerous arsenals without similar paperwork. It doesn't make sense.

Hang Around After You're Gone

The latest thing in jewelry, cremation pendants, won't be on everyone's wish list this Christmas. On my personal pleasure index, receiving one of the pendants would be similar to unwrapping a gift certificate for root canal work.

Actually, the cremation pendants make the most recent jewelry trend, body-piercing, look rather tame by comparison.

High-priced cremation jewelry, which stores loved ones' ashes in a locket-style pendant, will cost $1,900 to $10,000 and is now being sold exclusively at select funeral homes across the country. Available in heart, teardrop and cylinder shapes, the pendants are roughly two inches tall and come in white or yellow gold, with or without diamonds.

Grief Counselor Mary Lou Cook told the Wall Street Journal, "There are certain people who would feel really good about having the ashes of their loved ones accompany them all the time." Count me out, Mary Lou.

If the trend catches on, we may soon find the following classified ad in our newspapers: "Lost. Reward offered. Gold pendant. Answers to the name Bill."

The pendants would certainly add a new dimension to marriage proposals. Instead of saying, "Darling, as a token of my love, I would like you to wear my grandmother's ring", the prospective groom would declare, "As a token of my love, I would like you to wear my grandmother."

"I haven't anybody to wear!" would be the lament

of women everywhere as they dress for special occasions.

"This piece of jewelry has been in our family for years", would take on new meaning as family members become the baubles themselves.

The pendants might also become a form of sweet revenge upon the living. People who have been "pains in the neck" or "albatrosses around necks" for most of their lives would be able to continue doing the same thing after they're long gone.

As funeral directors and jewelry designers become interchangeable professions, it won't be uncommon to hear such comments as, "Your great-aunt goes perfectly with your blue dress!"

If wearing relatives' ashes becomes a common practice, it would be possible to "lose" someone more than once.

The pendants would also affect our judicial system. Pendant thieves could possibly be charged with two crimes simultaneously — theft and kidnapping.

I strongly believe that people should be able to get into the spirit of Christmas without facing the possibility of being placed in the gifts themselves. At the ends of our lives there must be something better than becoming a gift that keeps on giving.

The Six Stages Of Christmas

Forget the 12 days of Christmas. The Pillsbury Company in Minneapolis has extended the holiday season to 16 weeks. They have also gone through the bother of labeling holiday stress stages we are expected to experience during those weeks.

The first stage, Awareness, begins in early September. During this period of time we are aware that we will have to lose at least half our body weight to wear the same clothes we wore last Christmas, but we're not overly concerned. It's still too early to think about paying for gifts, updating Christmas card lists or locating cookbooks that were stashed away last January and haven't resurfaced.

During the second stage which begins in mid-October, Dreams, we begin fantasizing on a national scale about perfect holidays. With Martha Stewart as our role model, we know that we too will be able to weave gorgeous wreaths with grasses shipped in from the Argentine pampas. We begin clipping exotic recipes out of magazines and the local grocer promises to special order balsamic vinegar, pine nuts and sun-dried tomatoes for the gourmet turkey stuffing.

From Thanksgiving time through mid-December, we experience the third stage, Effort. We make the effort to stave off desserts for a couple of days and we buy 10 boxes of Christmas cards which will be addressed later. In spite of our efforts, the Argentinian government responds to our request for Pampas grass with a letter which appears to be written in another language, and the grocer calls with the bad news that pine nuts are out of season.

The fourth stage, Panic, begins in mid-December. The unopened boxes of Christmas cards have become dust collectors on the kitchen table, and the newspaper boy, a first-year Spanish student, tries to translate the letter from Argentina. So far, he has come up with "Dear Sir". Cases of balsmic vinegar and sun-dried tomatoes have turned the kitchen into an obstacle course and we have somehow misplaced the recipe requiring those ingredients. With the added stress, we have gained 10 pounds. The Christmas tree has settled with the warmth of the house and has taken over most of the living room. The only other tree left at the sales lot had two branches.

Enjoyment, the fifth stage, begins on December 24. In spite of the chaos surrounding us — an unidentified toddler wanders into the tree in the living room and becomes lost for several minutes and the bank calls to check if a recent buying frenzy was the result of a stolen credit card — we manage to laugh and smile. The Pampas grass wreath never happens.

The post-holiday stress period, Acceptance, allows us to accept the facts that all of our meals for the next year will include sun-dried tomatoes and balsamic vinegar, that Martha Stewart has a hired staff and that all of our bills for Christmas gifts will eventually be paid. Thanks to Pillsbury, we can also accept the knowledge that another Christmas is only eight months away.

Snow Shoveling Precautions

Consider them as late Christmas gifts from the Minnesota Chiropractic Association. That group has issued the following recommendations for those of us who aren't already limping around with snow-shoveling injuries. The words in parentheses are theirs.

(Dress warmly and cover your neck because cold air causes muscles to tighten leading to potential stress.) One word of caution, however. If you bundle up with too many layers of clothing, you might also fall face down into a snowbank and be unable to get up. As you flail your arms about, signalling for help, the neighbors driving by may think you're only having fun making snow angels.

(Stretch before shoveling.) Before venturing outdoors, stretch for a cookie jar or a sack of potato chips on a high shelf in the kitchen. By doing so, suitable exercise will be rewarded with instant gratification in the form of warmth-generating calories.

(Use scoop shovels to push instead of lift.) Better yet, break the scoop part of the shovel from the handle. This may be accomplished by using leverage on something sturdy, such as the bumper of a nearby car or the garage door's overhead track. No one would expect you to move snow with a broken shovel and it would serve as a perfect plea for help. Stand at the street end of your driveway with a shovel piece in each hand and a sad, forlorn look on your face. Think "snowstorm poster child" and help will be on the way.

(Don't throw shovelsful while you're bent over. Bend more with the knees than with the hips.) This sounds like exercise, but it does justify several more trips back to the cookie jar and potato chips. Although the exact numbers aren't available, assume that lifting one shovelful of snow burns off 15,000 calories.

(Switch hands every five scoops.) Presumably, those switched hands will belong to a spouse, one of your offspring or a kindly stranger, not unlike Clint Eastwood's character in "The Bridges of Madison County". If the hand-switching works, you might find yourself cast in the movie's sequel, "The Snowbanks of Whatever County".

(Don't do too much at once.) Although shoveling your driveway might become a three-day task, break up the monotony with frequent naps, snacks and idle daydreams about trading the house for a 32-foot motor home and moving to Florida or Texas.

Ralph Waldo Emerson once wrote, "The four months of snow make the inhabitants of the northern temperate zones wiser and abler." Those months also make them more creative when faced with the harsh realities of shoveling snow.

Good Intentions

My apologies to Samuel Johnson, but the road to a blizzard is also paved with good intentions. The following notes, written while a snowstorm swept through our region a few weeks ago, have resurfaced.

Day 1: Good news! The TV weatherman announced rather excitedly tonight that a blizzard is headed our way and will make its presence known during the next few hours. I love snow days! With no meetings to attend, no trips to town and no possibility of leaving the house for at least 24 hours, I feel like the prisoner who has been given a last minute reprieve by the governor! What glorious freedom!

I've already written a list of things to do tomorrow. In not necessarily this order, I will reorganize my address book, read a great American novel and, if time permits, I will write one. The shelf paper I bought in 1962 will be located and the kitchen cupboards will look like something out of Better Homes and Gardens magazine. The family photo albums, which haven't been touched in years, will be updated. I will make a real dinner for my family and I will start my diet. In anticipation of the big storm, all I ate tonight was a lettuce salad with non-fat dressing and half a can of tuna. I feel thinner already!

Day 2: It's a blizzard, all right. According to the weather reports, the wind is gusting at 50 miles an hour and the wind chill is 60 degrees below zero. The world outside has disappeared because of the white-outs. There's an eight-foot drift between our garage and the road.

Woke up early to start the day, but fell asleep again after the first two pages of "The Grapes of Wrath". Finished the title page of my novel after I woke up to the sound of voices on the TV. Victoria Newman on "The Young and the Restless" wants to leave her husband for another man. I lost all sense of time as three other soap operas appeared on the screen, followed by Oprah and Rosie. Failed to locate shelf paper, address book or photo albums during the commercials. Baked a frozen pizza for the family. Today I finished off the can of tuna and half a bag of Oreos. The blizzard warning has been extended to another day. I've gained two pounds.

Day 3: Reread the first two pages of "The Grapes of Wrath" at 6 a.m. The title page of my novel had to be retyped because the other one had a coffee ring. Nothing but white outside the windows, and the rooms in the house seem smaller for some reason. The winds have blown the TV antenna out of position so all we can get is a snowy picture on the screen. Kept staring at the screen for four hours, hoping something would appear. For dinner tonight fed the family do-it-yourself peanut butter and jelly sandwiches. After eating the remaining Oreos and their crumbs, a gallon of ice-cream, two boxes of crackers and a couple of houseplants, which fortunately proved to be non-toxic, I wasn't very hungry. The diet must be working.

Day 4: The winds stopped during the night, and the snowplow opened our road. The living room appears to be the size of a postage stamp. I'm going to town. As for the address book, the photo albums, the kitchen shelves, the diet and the novels, there will always be another snowstorm.

To Tip Or Not To Tip

According to a study at Cornell University, leaving tips at restaurants has become a complicated matter. If the study is accurate, waiters and waitresses are giving us subliminal messages which will determine how much loose cash will be left on the table at the end of the meal.

By drawing a happy face on the back of a restaurant check, a waitress will scoop up an average 18 percent more in tips when the table is cleared than if she had merely scribbled, "Thanks! Tracy." The implication of the smiling face is that lugging trays of food to your table has been an exhilarating experience for her, not unlike flying to the moon or giving birth to triplets. Her enthusiasm is conveyed to the customers and they dig deeper into their wallets.

Drawing a last-minute circle with two dots for eyes and a loopy smile can actually be more profitable than spending one's life as a struggling artist or a forger of art masterpieces.

On the other hand, male waiters who draw whimsical happy faces on the backs of their checks are likely to receive three percent less in tips. The idea of having a light-hearted waiter who draws cartoon faces is evidently a turnoff for most diners.

The study also noted that when male waiters "casually touch a customer on the shoulder or hand, especially when the customer is female", their tips will rise substantially — in most cases, 42 percent.

Newspaper accounts of the study failed to mention other food serving behaviors which also result in smaller than usual tips.

My husband and I enjoy getting dressed up and going out for dinner. In my case, getting dressed up means wiggling into ill-fitting pantyhose and high heeled shoes and doing the face thing with lipstick and other camouflage materials.

When we are finally seated at a table in a nice restaurant, the waiter or waitress appears and asks, "What do youse guys want?" This may not seem like an insult to some people, but being addressed as a guy when you're trussed up like a Thanksgiving turkey and trying to project a feminine image really puts a damper on the evening. Treating a woman like one of the guys is hardly the way to pave the way to financial security and eventual retirement.

The second type of low-tip behavior involves sharing more information than the diner can digest about your personal life. This would include showing billfold photos of your pets and children and revealing certain medical facts. Not every restaurant customer is interested in seeing the film from a recent CAT-scan or an appendectomy scar. Such facts can cast a pall over an entire evening, if not lend a different taste to the main entree.

The study also failed to mention the waiter who rushes to your table and announces, "Hi! I'm Harold and I will be with you this evening." This introduction is unsettling for customers who ordinarily dislike drop-in company and raises all sorts of questions. Once the main course is served, will Harold pull up an extra chair and join us? Did we come into this restaurant to eat or did we hope to begin a long-lasting relationship with a third person?

The simple act of ordering from a menu and enjoying a meal shouldn't carry with it a promise of exchanging names or addresses with the person doing the serving. Ordering the special of the day shouldn't result in sending Harold Christmas or birthday cards.

When it comes to having a waiter "casually touching" his hand or shoulder while he is eating, I am fairly certain my husband will leave no tip at all.

Ice Fisherman – Our Next Astronauts

A future astronaut, waiting for his first journey into space, has become a fixture in our novels and movies. The character Will in "Independence Day" is an excellent example of an astronaut wannabe.

However, little has been said or written about the noble Americans who have been training for years to be the first settlers on the moon. I refer, of course, to ice fishermen from the Upper Midwest, who are already acclimated to harsh temperatures and barren surroundings which resemble lunar landscapes.

While the rest of us assumed the ice fishermen were only angling for fish, trying to keep warm and giving up quality time with their families, the fishermen must have known they had a greater purpose. That purpose was revealed recently when the Defense Department announced that Clementine, a military spacecraft, had found possible ice ponds on the dark side of the moon.

Furthermore, the Defense Department believes that the discovery increases the chance that humans will live on the moon someday. Creating homes for moon ice pond settlements shouldn't be a problem. Their designs have been on the drawing boards for years.

Constructed of relatively inexpensive materials, the lunar homes will resemble the ice houses found on our lakes. Created from long abandoned outhouses, travel trailers and grain silos, the ice houses are clear evidence of man's ingenuity and resourcefulness.

I can't speak for others, but it would be wonderful if the moon's first inhabitants wore caps reading, "A bad day of fishing is better than a good day at the office" or T-shirts proclaiming, "Anglers do it in the water."

Ice fishermen will be perfect candidates for the first moon settlement. They are already accustomed to sitting for hours in the middle of vast wastelands. A few months on the moon would pass like the blink of an eye for those stalwart sportsmen who are already used to ice fishing for the six long months of a midwestern winter.

The austere isolation of the lunar landscape wouldn't pose a problem for the ice anglers, either. After they've adjusted to the the dark interior of a fish house, with nothing but a pole, a space heater and stale sandwiches for company, they keep their socializing to a minimum. Talking with an ice fisherman, while he's mesmerized by a hole in the floorboards of his ice house, can be an unsettling experience.

"Catching anything?"
"Yep."
"Any big ones?"
"Yep."
"Anything exciting going on?"
"Froze three toes last month."

Watching an ice fisherman staring at a hole in a frozen lake is similar to watching a guy staring at a blank television screen without a remote control in his hand. Time tends to stand still.

The prospect of setting up an ice house on a lunar pond which stays frozen for 365 days a year will be an irresistible temptation for many fishermen. And if the fish aren't biting? That's all right, too.

Blizzard Braggadocio

Because of the wind chill factors, only one competition is reaching a fevered pitch these days. Officially, the game, which pits neighbor against neighbor and friend against friend, is called Blizzard Braggadocio. For the sake of people who are unable to pronounce Italian-sounding words with frozen tongues, we'll call it Blizzard Bragging.

The rules for playing are simple. A person who escapes a blizzard relatively unscathed is an automatic loser. While playing the game this week with a formidable opponent — she said the only entrance to her house was as wide as a shovel and I countered that the only entrance to our house was the overhead garage door — a third friend broke her silence.

"I hate to admit this," she stammered, "but we don't have any snowdrifts on our yard."

The distrained look we gave her was one ordinarily reserved for serial killers or people who confess to cleaning behind their stoves and refrigerators.

Competition in Blizzard Bragging centers on four categories: visual effects, damage to personal property, physical pain and mental anguish. Points are recorded as the players blurt out their hardships from the most recent snowstorm.

When it comes to visual effects, having a car buried completely under the snow or having house windows half-covered with snow drifts pale by comparison when someone mentions that the fuel oil company can't locate his fuel tank under a 30-foot, rock-hard snowdrift and the last time he looked the needle gauge was nearing empty. Life-threatening visual effects are always trump cards.

In the category of damage to personal property, a deck loaded with five-foot snowdrifts and threatening to break off from the house and roll into a nearby ravine would lose to a house roof which has completely collapsed. In this case, a person with a television antenna lying across a kitchen table and shingles strewn all over the beds would definitely be a winner.

Physical pain competition can involve having facial features — eyelids, nostrils or even a mouth — frozen shut for extended periods of time. Even a combination of having all three facial features frozen can't compete with having a nose falling off one's face because of the bitter cold or having a foot amputated. Extra points are awarded, however, for bringing back feeling to frozen toes and fingers.

When dealing with snow shoveling injuries, sustaining a ruptured disk has a definite advantage over a sprained muscle when the final scores are compared.

Mental anguish is the broadest category. In this event, being stranded in your own house with no place to go for at least 48 hours loses to being stranded in a complete stranger's house for the same length of time. If that stranger is completely covered with tattoos and a motorcycle is parked in his living room, extra points are gained.

However, a hands-down winner in the stranded situation would have to be parents confined to a house with four children under the age of five. If those same parents have gone without electricity, water or telephone service, they are automatically given championship status.

Giving birth to a baby in a snowbank can only be surpassed by being stranded in a house for three days without coffee, chocolate and potato chips. When it comes to one-upmanship in its purest form, nothing can beat Blizzard Bragging. Let the playing continue!

Promiscuous Fishing

The Department of Natural Resources (DNR) people in our area may be opening up a whole new can of worms. They announced last week that "promiscuous or unlimited fishing" will be allowed on three local lakes until February 28 because of a heavy ice and snow cover.

As a result, fish, car trunksful of them, "may be taken by any means except the use of electricity, toxicants and/or explosive devices". This eliminates the possibility of catching fish by felling power poles into lakes, emptying last week's lethal coffee onto the ice outside a fishing house or employing nuclear bombs. Anything else is fair play.

The term in the press release that confused me the most was "promiscuous fishing". Does this refer to the fisherman, the sport of fishing itself or the fish?

Assuming it's the latter, we have known about the moral integrity of fish for sometime now. Why else would we have negative expressions such as "fish story" or "there's something fishy about this"? "A fish in troubled waters" is also viewed negatively as an opportunist who thrives during other people's misfortunes.

Promiscuous fishing will allow us to deal with fish on their own shady terms. By spinning ice augers in the opposite direction than they usually go, we will be able to make first contacts with the fish by relaying raunchy, subliminal messages.

After the holes are drilled in the ice, we will be able to lure the fish out of the water by waving pinup posters of naked minnows and nightcrawlers before their eyes, appealing to their baser instincts. Within gill distance of the fish, we will be able to recite bawdy limericks, beginning with first lines such as "There once was a perch from Pawtucket."

We will tempt them out of the holes in the ice with bawdy jokes, stories and songs. Because of the promiscuous nature of fish, they will be jumping out of the water and into our frying pans once they have heard a joke beginning, "There was this crappie that walked into a bar..." or "Who was that northern pike I saw you with last night?" Shaggy fish stories will also prove useful.

Without restrictions on our fishing, unsafe angling will no longer be taboo. Instead of loading our hooks with traditional bait, we will be able to bait our lines with objects that entice our own species — greasy chunks of pepperoni pizza, lottery tickets and the greatest temptation of all, chocolate chips. We will literally have the fish eating out of our hands.

A spokesman for the DNR noted, "Instead of wasting a resource, we are lifting the restrictions so fishermen can get some good from it." With unrestricted, promiscuous fishing techniques, the fish will presumably have some fun, too.

The Tree-Cutting Chromosome

According to Mason Weems, author of the 1800 bestseller, "Life of Washington", six-year-old George Washington once confessed, "I can't tell a lie, Pa, you know I can't tell a lie. I did cut it with my hatchet." Weems's book about our first president was so popular that 59 editions were published between 1800 and 1850.

Washington's birthday will be celebrated this month, and many historians are pooh-poohing the legend about the young future president chopping down an English cherry tree and his refusal to lie about the incident.

In spite of their protests, I believe young George did chop down the tree. I also believe that a certain chromosome in people, particularly males, can be linked to the inherent desire to cut down trees and watch them fall. In those people, the tree-cutting chromosome is located somewhere between the chromosome that doesn't permit a person to ask for directions when lost and the chromosome that gives a person absolute dominion over a TV remote control.

In other people, mostly females, this troublesome cluster of chromosomes is replaced by chromosomes that make it impossible for them to reveal their true weights and ages and to accept their natural hair colors. Tree-cutting and fictional weights — in the end they balance each other.

The person with a chainsaw in our house was called into action on a recent winter day. I can't be sure, but I thought I could hear his chromosomes singing their own version of Hendel's "Hallelujah Chorus" when I told him about the visit from the TV satellite dish installer.

"The dead cottonwood tree will have to be sawed down before we can have the dish installed," I told the man with the chainsaw. "It's blocking the signal."

"Is that so?" Translation: "Hallelujah!"

"It has to come down before Friday."

"Okay." Hallelu, hallelu, hallelujah!

Apparently there's one thing more exciting than cutting down a tree and feeling its branches rush past your ears as the tree plummets to the ground. That's being ordered by a satellite dish company to cut down a tree.

A smile spread over the chainsawer's face. It was the smile that might also appear on the face of an airplane passenger when he's told that the pilot and co-pilot have succumbed to food poisoning and that the passengers have chosen him to land the plane. It was the smile of a person facing a formidable challenge.

Within seconds he disappeared into the dark depths of our attached garage, and he could be heard murmuring, "She's been around for about 25 years now. I hope the old girl still has some kick left in her." I only hoped he was referring to the chainsaw.

The tree came down without incident. As I watched it fall to the ground and shatter into thousands of lifeless pieces, I also thought about people with chainsaw chromosomes. By varying somewhat the popular slogan of Smokey, the fire fighting bear, they truly believe only they can prevent forests.

Charter Plane Trips

We weren't wide-eyed innocents. When my husband and I traveled to the Dominican Republic recently, we fully expected to see hardships, discomfort and generally unpleasant living conditions.

However, we had no idea that all of those elements would occur within minutes after taking off from the Minneapolis airport. When it came to suffering, the Caribbean country paled by comparison.

Our plane was owned by a charter tour company, and the 200-plus seats originally installed on the DC-10 soon after the big war had been replaced by 400 seats. The latter were roughly the size of infant car seats, designed for persons with hips no wider than 20 inches and legs the length of those normally found on a Barbie doll.

Charter plane seats favor function over comfort, and the obligatory seat belts are totally unnecessary. Once a person is wedged into an assigned seat, with arms pinned to his sides and knees tucked under his chin, there's little chance of becoming dislodged. After remaining in that position for five hours, it's apparent to the passenger that relief is spelled c-r-o-w-b-a-r.

Relatively simple tasks, such as reading and eating, became insurmountable challenges. After a couple of hours of reading, I realized that my pinioned arms had lost all sensation below the elbows, and that my chances of turning over a page were about the same as appearing onstage at Carnegie Hall.

It was also our misfortune to be seated behind the most heinous fellow travelers of all, the much dreaded Recliners. Without giving thought to the comfort of the passengers seated behind them, the Recliners leaned back in their seats and became part of our lives. For most of the trip my husband learned more about male balding patterns than he had ever hoped to learn. With the Recliner's shiny pate only inches from his face, my husband, by that time in what appeared to be the final stages of rigor mortis, had studied enough to become a self-taught phrenologist.

My female Recliner, on the other hand, had large masses of hair. From my vantage point, two inches from her flowing mane, she would have been a shoo-in winner in any Farrah Fawcett look-alike contest. Even in her sleep the Recliner would toss her tresses from side to side. That in itself wasn't a problem until the meals were served.

Eating shriveled peas, cold mashed potatoes and some unidentifiable meat with a thin plastic fork was challenging enough with my arms fused permanently to my ribs. What made the act of eating most difficult was locating the main entree beneath the Recliner's cascading hair and synchronizing my fork lifting with her hair tossing.

Of course, the main benefit to traveling on a charter plane is the great savings. For most people it's no longer necessary to mortgage the house or dip into retirement funds to travel from a cold place to a warm place during the winter. The possibility is great, however, that those savings will be spent on prescriptions for muscle relaxants and pain relievers and trips to the doctor's office.

The Downside Of Cloning Ourselves

Many people, the First Lady included, have been telling us that it takes a entire village to raise a child. It now appears that it will take a small group to have one.

Dolly, the sheep recently cloned by a Scottish scientist, is the collaborative effort of three sheep. By taking DNA tissue from one ewe, fusing it with an unfertilized egg from a second ewe, and then having a third ewe carry the embryo to term, Dr. Ian Wilmut of the Roslin Institute has created a perfect duplicate of the original donor.

In one sense, science has taken one step backward. Previously, only two sheep were required to produce a lamb. It now requires three. Reproduction isn't normally a group activity.

Although the procedure is undoubtedly expensive, we can only wonder what would happen if humans would begin cloning themselves. It's possible that a parent would someday tell his offspring, "Back in the old days, we were so poor, our parents had to make babies the old-fashioned way."

It's also interesting that three ewes were used in the project, neatly eliminating the need for a male, a candlelight dinner and soft music playing in the background. Carried to an extreme, we could possibly become a civilization cursed by clogged kitchen drains, cars that won't function, piles of trash that haven't been carried out and unshoveled snowbanks. We must proceed cautiously with this cloning business.

The father and mother name blanks on birth certificates and birth announcement cards and in baby books would have to be changed to include new designations: DNA donor, egg donor and surrogate carrier. Even simple nursery songs would have to be reworded — "Bye baby bunting, donor's gone a-hunting."

Conceivably, pun intended, cloning could result in traditional all-female households. Instead of being told that they're special and one of a kind, children would learn that they're one of a dozen or so.

In a world of cloning, we would be able to tell a mother her baby looks exactly like her and mean it. Sons would no longer be referred to as chips off the old block — they would be the old block. There would no be no need for speculations about which parent a baby resembles.

With three or four look-alike clones doing the work for one woman, super-moms would no longer be distinguishable.

Criminal trials, just coming into their own with conclusive DNA evidence, would become a thing of the past. With so many identical DNA combinations, fingerprints and physical appearances on the loose, it would be difficult to identify a single felon.

In such a case, the judge would have to sing out, "Send in the clones."

Sound Advice For Young Adults

Advice books for young singles, written by single people, are selling like proverbial hotcakes. The best-selling titles include "The Rules", "The Real Rules", "Breaking the Rules" and "The Code: Time-Tested Secrets for Getting What You Want From Women — Without Marrying Them".

Based on mating rituals, which supposedly have been discovered by Generation X, the books advise singles on all aspects of dating and eventual trips to the altar. One book even deals with dating the dead, according to a recent article in the Los Angeles Tribune. In "Astral Love", D.J. Conway's readers are told how to attract sweethearts from the spirit realm.

The only angle missing, of course, is a rule book written for singles by their parents. After all, we're the advice experts. For starters, the following rules could be explained:

Rule One: If you must move somewhere with a new job, move to a warm climate. We will enjoy visiting you for long extended periods during the winter months. Our bathing suits and denture creams are already packed.

Rule Two: It's the gift, not the thought, that counts. Now that you're receiving regular paychecks, forget what we told you when you used to give us plaster casts of your tiny hands made in grade school, limp bunches of dandelions and stones from the driveway. In case you're wondering, we've been thinking VCRs and large screen TVs.

Rule Three: Your parents will always be there for

you — if they're not golfing, vacationing or doing something else. Your parents are only a voice mail or answering machine away.

Rule Four: In most states, the statute of limitations on storage of high school memorabilia is four years. This would be a good time to reclaim your old prom dresses, high school yearbooks, dried-up corsages, letters from friends you met at summer camps and your collection of stuffed animals.

Rule Four: Contrary to what Thomas Wolfe said, you can go home again — but your parents will be at their new condo.

Rule Five: The letters "OD" (overdrawn) on a returned check do not mean "Opt for Dad". Also "NSF" (non-sufficient funds) does not mean "Need to Speak to Father."

Rule Six: If you should glance into a mirror in the near future and see one of us staring back at you, don't scream or think your life is over. Becoming one's parents is a natural phenomenon. We went through the same thing as we grew older.

Unfortunately, a parent's list of rules wouldn't include timely advice about dating and courtship. By the time our children are young adults, we've forgotten how it was done.

The Deadly Mongoose

Before my husband and I left for our vacation a few weeks ago, a well-meaning friend advised, "You're going to the Dominican Republic? You'd better see your doctor. I heard there's a bad virus going around down there."

Bad virus. The words sent shivers down my spine. You don't have to be a research scientist to know that bad viruses, specifically fatal viruses, kill more people than any other kind.

Because my total knowledge about deadly viruses is the result of watching Dustin Hoffman in "Outbreak" at least 10 times and reading about biological weapons in Stephen King's "The Stand", I decided to seek out the advice of trained professionals.

A county health nurse in Iowa referred me to a regional health nurse in Sioux City. The latter was unable to field phone calls because she was sick at home, a fact I found rather disconcerting. According to my phone calls, at least half of the U.S. population could already have the bad virus.

My fears mounted when I called the Minnesota Department of Health. Between bouts with a hacking cough, their spokesperson told me to call the automated phone system of the national Center for Disease Control in Atlanta.

"Thank you for calling the CDC", droned the mechanical answering service. "For serious diseases in the southern hemisphere punch #1 on your phone. For the northern hemisphere touch #2." By narrowing the choices and punching a few more times, I finally located the Caribbean islands.

"In the Dominican Republic rabies, at times fatal, is being spread by the mongoose," the voice continued. "For more information about rabies, touch #1 on your touchtone phone. For additional diseases, touch #2."

The mongoose. Because of the mechanical woman's wording, I didn't know if one mongoose was raising havoc on the island or if the CDC was uncertain about the plural for mongoose and was playing it safe.

"For information about Hepatitis A, touch #1..."

What would the plural be? Mongoose, mongooses or mongeese?

"For information about Hepatitis B, touch #2..."

While I pondered about the nature of plural nouns, the mechanical voice recited its litany of deadly diseases.

"For information about malaria, touch #1. For information about typhoid fever, touch #2..."

Would I recognize a mongoose if I were to meet one face to face? Do mongooses/mongeese resemble cats or some mixed breed of dog? Petting a rabid mongoose under the mistaken notion that it was a terrier-dachshund cross would certainly put a damper on our vacation plans.

"For information about salmonella, touch #3..."

As the voice on the phone droned on, I looked up mongoose in the encyclopedia. The fuzzy photo accompanying the article showed a furry animal with sharp teeth. My eyes dropped down to the words, "It has a fierce disposition, but can be easily tamed." Our vacation itinerary didn't allow for an animal with a bad attitude.

"For information about hepatitis, touch #4." I hung up the phone. It's true, you know, what Chuang-Tzu, the Chinese philosopher, said — much knowledge is a curse. It's also entirely possible to know more than you understand.

White House Guests - Who Cares?

Poll-takers and certain members of the media seem surprised that Americans aren't bothered by the White House houseguest controversy.

We don't seem to care that as many as 938 overnight guests, many of them major contributors, have been entertained by the First Family. It doesn't bother us to hear that kings, princes, Richard Dreyfuss, Billy Graham and Steven Spielberg have slept in the Lincoln Bedroom.

We may appear to be apathetic, but actually we have been quietly mulling the situation over in our minds. We think and we plan. How wrong can it be to have houseguests who leave generous donations behind? That's a much better alternative than having overnight guests who only leave a pile of dirty towels and a sinkful of unwashed dishes.

According to an article in a bank's newsletter, a national broker franchise recently asked its affiliates to give valuations of the White House in Washington, DC. The average current value of the 42,840 square foot home, located on 18 acres of prime, downtown DC land came to $63,893,550.

In order to own such a house a buyer would need to slap down $6,389,355 for a down payment, have $25.7 million in qualifying annual income and pay $600,000 in monthly house payments.

Given those numbers, it's not surprising that White House guests have been leaving behind relatively small tokens of their appreciation. It's the least they can do.

For all we know, this paying houseguest trend may soon spread to our own homes. In addition to boosting our personal incomes, houseguest contributions would certainly take large bites out of our mortgage payments. Our master bedrooms could be reserved for the highest bidders. Guests asking for special amenities, such as clean bedsheets, spare toothbrushes or something to eat, would be required to pay for those services.

Houseguests unable or unwilling to contribute financially would be required to paint the exterior of the house, cut and stack firewood for the following winter, weed the garden or re-seed the lawn. We would welcome those guests with open arms, although photo opportunities with the hosts, of course, would cost extra.

Although the guest sleeping quarters in our homes aren't qualified to be called the Queen's Room or the Lincoln Bedroom, they could be referred to as the Alley View Room, the Washer and Dryer Room or the Furnace Room. Those designations alone would give the rooms a touch of class.

On the other hand, if this White House overnight guest controversy doesn't go away, the President might choose to follow the example set by a New Hampshire farmer many years ago. Daniel Webster, according to folklore, was once hunting in his native state, some distance from the inn where he had been staying, and rather than make the long trip back, he approached a farmhouse after dark and pounded on the door.

An upstairs window was finally raised and the farmer called out, "What do you want?"

"I want to spend the night here," said Webster.

"All right. Stay there," replied the farmer. Down went the window.

Winter Amnesia

Contrary to popular belief, the Upper Midwest has five seasons. The fifth is a black, gray and white time in the spring before leaves appear on trees and shrubs and the countryside turns green. It's the time before rains wash away the dirty residue of winter and last autumn's leaves seem permanently plastered to driveways and lawns.

The fifth season also marks the onset of widespread cases of winter amnesia. We forget what winter was like and we don't remember again until the next winter rolls around. Only weeks ago, while our gloves were frozen to the handles of snow shovels and our brains were numbed by the cold, we told ourselves, "This weather is too much. I'll relocate to a warmer part of the country." Like a woman who has given birth for the first time we declared, "I will never go through this again."

Forgetting so quickly a winter that lasted six months shouldn't be that easy. In terms of many human relationships, six months is a rather long time.

The giddiness we experience during this fifth season can be identified by the way we swagger through the streets with our coats unzipped and our heads uncovered. We appear to have been drinking from the Lethe (rhymes with teethy), the river of forgetfulness in Greek and Roman mythology.

In addition to softening the memories of the past winter, we also managed to forget what our lawns and surroundings looked like before the first snow came and the winds began to howl. The longer we stood at our windows during the winter months and stared out at the knee-deep snow covering our yards, the more perfect our imagined surroundings became.

During the winter our lawns had become glamorized in our minds. Before the snows came, we had raked the lawn, cleaned out the garden, removed the neighbor's dog's droppings and put away the volleyball net. With the appearance of the fifth season, we discover that we had done none of those things.

As the thick blanket of snow disappears, we begin to re-orientate ourselves and play a mind-sharpening game called "What's that?" What's that? Why, that's the grill. What's that? That's the lawnmower. No, it's the picnic table.

The lawns we vaguely remembered during the long winter months seem quite foreign when they reappear. By the time the snow has nearly disappeared, and all we have left are a few banks caked with dirt blown in from Wyoming and Montana, we wistfully miss the snow. It covered a multitude of imperfections.

As we look out the windows, where the views were for the longest time obliterated by snowdrifts, we actually miss the familiar whiteness. Caught up in the throes of winter amnesia, we remember fondly how the first snows last fall signalled the end of washing windows, mowing the lawn and filling another dozen quart jars with tomatoes from the garden.

The snow had become a great, white equalizer and the lawns of rich and poor looked the same. Every farm yard appeared to be the subject of a Currier and Ives print.

Without winter amnesia, few of us would live here.

Lifestyles Of The Rich And Not So Rich

In his story, "Rich Boy", F. Scott Fitzgerald wrote, "Let me tell you about the very rich. They are different from you and me." The people he wrote about were undoubtedly interested in the annual Moet Luxury Index, which was released a few weeks ago by LVNH Moet Hennessey Louis Vuitton SA, the world's largest luxury goods maker.

The index claims to gauge the inflation rate for the "cost of REALLY living" by tracking the prices of 12 luxury items. Incidentally, none of the items on the list are available at the local Walmart, so don't bother looking.

According to the report, the prices of Rolex Oyster watches and Teuscher imported chocolate truffles haven't changed during the past year. However, the index rose when round-trip Concorde tickets were increased to $8,226 and the cost of a full-length mink coat jumped to $19,000. Adding insult to injury, a Rolls-Royce Silver Spur now carries a price tag of $186,100. These are indeed troublesome days.

My most recent brush with Moet Index-type people happened three weeks ago, when I accompanied my husband on a business trip to Omaha and we stayed at a relatively posh hotel. It wasn't the kind of place where you pull up to the entrance and someone in the car, usually the husband, says, "I know it's not fancy, but all we need is a clean room and a good bed."

For that reason, I am submitting this Fancy Hotel Room Index. You know you're with Fitzgerald's people when:

All of the other names on the guest register don't read "Mr. and Mrs. Smith" and there's no sign at the front desk indicating hourly rates.

The desk clerk refers to you as a guest, not a "stranger in these parts." The registration card at the front desk doesn't require you to name your next of kin.

You don't leave your car in a parking lot with a sign reading, "Park at your own risk."

You aren't asked to pay your bill in advance.

The bath towels in the room are so thick that when they're taken as souvenirs, guests can't close their suitcases.

You fall asleep knowing that each hour of sleep is costing you $15. You can go broke sleeping.

You don't know the first names of the strangers in the next room because the walls are so thin.

The art prints, lamps and TV in the room aren't bolted firmly in place.

The drinking glasses aren't covered with plastic wrap and they're made of real glass, not plastic.

The TV isn't the focal point of the room. In fact, it's hidden in its own cabinet and you might have to call the front desk to pinpoint its exact location.

You find a chocolate mint on the bed pillow, not a brochure titled, "What to do if your Life is Threatened." In addition, the pillows don't feel like cement blocks.

The Gideon Bible in the night stand hasn't been stolen by a previous occupant.

Earlier guests haven't carved their initials or phone numbers on the bed's headboard.

The room has a closet, not three wire clothes hangers suspended from the ceiling light fixture.

Last but not least, you know you're staying in a really fancy place when it takes three or four credit cards to pay your bill when you check out.

How To Handle Overdue Letters

Social letter-writing has become a lost art. This fact became painfully evident recently when I found a stack of unanswered letters under a layer of dust.

After noticing that most of the envelopes carried 29-cent stamps, I realized I was facing an insurmountable task. Who were these correspondents from a buried past? Were they still alive? Would the ex-student who wrote still be in college 15 years later? Is there a statue of limitations regarding unanswered letters?

What used to be a national pastime — covering crisp, white linen paper with the joyful flourish of pen and ink — has given way to guilt and fear. The guilt surfaces when a letter goes unanswered for days, weeks or even years. The only thing to be feared more than writing a long, overdue letter is writing a lettr and having it answered within 24 hours. Writing to someone who responds too quickly can result in a vicious cycle.

Anatole Broyard once remarked, "In an age like ours, which is not given to letter-writing, we forget what an important part it used to play in people's lives."

Of course, we must remember that when letter-writing was at its peak of popularity, people were also excited about getting the week's delivery of ice or being the first people on their block with indoor plumbing. In their slower paced world, they didn't have telephones, let alone faxes and E-mail.

As I tackled the old letters for the better part of a day,

I jotted down a few guidelines and letter-starters which might help others facing the same dilemma.

Guideline #1: Always refer to the other person's latest letter. Examples might be:

"Your letter recently resurfaced on my desk. In it, you noted that you were going to vote for Richard Nixon in the upcoming election..."

"It doesn't seem possible that your little girl is 19 and most likely in college! I found her birth announcement yesterday while cleaning off my desk..."

"Dear John: Thanks for your letter which outlined our incredible future together. I'm writing to inform you that I married another person 35 years ago..."

"Thank you for the kind invitation to your Tupperware party. Even though 10 years have passed, is it too late to order a lettuce crisper?"

"Merry Christmas to you, too! I hope that all your wishes for the new year, 1992, came true..."

Guideline #2: Minimize, if possible, the tardiness of your reply. Examples of minimizing might include:

"Perhaps eight years may seem like a long time to you, but I have leftovers in my refrigerator even older than that..."

"What is time, anyway? When we stop to consider that the earth is millions of years old, an unanswered letter from 1984 seems fairly recent by comparison..."

The letters were finally written and mailed off. Although I may sound like a woman who has just given birth, I will never go through that again. From now on, I will follow the advice of Sir Francis Bacon, who wrote, "It is generally better to deal by speech than by letter." Instead of writing letters, I will use the phone.

My Time With The Phone Psychic

Sharon places a high value on our relationship - $2.95 a minute, to be exact. She works for a 900-psychic hotline which is often advertised on late night television. On a recent night my entertainment and purchasing choices were very limited — I could either talk with some stranger across the country about my future or I could order a set of cut-through-anything knives.

Because there were no car tires, sheets of steel or tomatoes in the house in desperate need of being sliced as thin as paper, I opted for the psychic.

Aware that the psychic phonelines are for-profit ventures and that the longer they can keep a customer on the phone, the more money they will make, I set down two rules before calling. The phone call wouldn't last longer than four minutes and I wouldn't waste time revealing details about my life. After all, a psychic would know all of those things and I wouldn't want to insult his or her intelligence.

At 11:05 Sharon introduced herself and asked for my name and birthdate. She then asked, "Do you have any special interests or problems?"

"Not really. How does my summer look?"

"Um...let's see...my reading is weak, but late May or early June should be more active and fulfilling. There might be some travel involved. The financial picture looks good." She paused, as if waiting for more information.

"You work, right?"

"Yes."

"Excellent! It's much clearer now. You will see some surprising developments during the last half of May. Yes! There is a definite promotion in your future!"

In the world of psychics a little knowledge can be a dangerous thing. Sharon had no way of knowing that the chance of a newspaper columnist being promoted is virtually non-existent.

At 11:09 Sharon's vision had disappeared. By the time we hung up, I realized that I had had much more interesting calls with telemarketers or with people reaching the wrong number. Relaying information from a mystical realm or the great beyond must be challenging work.

Following Sharon's lead, I've worked up the following readings for anyone who might be reading this:

Barring unforeseen circumstances, you will definitely observe a birthday sometime this year. There might or might not be a party.

Some of the days in June will be cloudy; the other days will be sunny.

A large tree will very likely appear in your living room in December.

Your hair and fingernails will continually grow during the upcoming months.

The sun will rise and set everyday.

You will experience good days and bad days during the upcoming year. Unless you're feeling sick, you will feel relatively healthy.

That will be $8.85. By the way, thanks for the promotion.

Gardening Blues

Frank Swinnerton once observed, "When you have done your best for a flower, and it fails, you have some reason to be aggrieved." If that is true, I should be wearing black for most of the summer. During the unusually cold month of May I was responsible for the premature demise of hundreds of flower and tomato plants.

In what turned out to be widespread planticide in our part of the country, I wasn't the only gardener who planted impatiens and Big Boys at least two or three times. During May, when 60 degree days repeatedly became 20 degree nights, I made more trips to the greenhouse to replace dead plants than I care to remember.

After the third such trip, one of the sales clerks looked at me and exclaimed, "You're back!"

I laughed nervously. "Yes — (heh! heh!) — a person can never have too many tomato plants."

"This weather has really been good for business," she responded. "Repeat customers like you have been coming in everyday."

I hadn't intended to be a serial plant killer. If it's true that parents only spend 15 minutes a day with their children in meaningful conversations, I spent more time this year with plants than I ever spent with my own children.

For weeks before the recommended planting time, I exhausted long morning hours lugging boxes of plants from the house and garage out into the sun. The same amount of time was devoted to carrying them back inside at nightfall. The heavy mileage from house to yard, back and forth for several weeks, took a heavy toll on the first group of plants and they made more trips outdoors than a dog with a weak bladder. The plants actually appeared to be growing smaller, if such a thing is possible.

I made the mistake of planting according to the calendar, fully aware that the last freezing date for our region was Mothers Day, an ordinarily upbeat occasion. The fledgling plants were doomed from the very minute their roots touched the cold ground. The frozen nightcrawlers I uncovered should have been a warning signal.

The second batch of flower and tomato plants, purchased one week later, met a more violent end. They had their necks broken and they suffocated when they were covered with blankets from every bed in the house. From the air our yard must have resembled a patchwork quilt, with blankets of all colors and old bedspreads covering the entire terrain. Countless hours were devoted to removing and replacing blankets and the rocks and other weights which held them down.

The broken neck and asphyxiation victims were replaced by a third batch of plants on Memorial Day Weekend. They are still alive, but they haven't grown substantially. At their present rate of growth, we should have bright blooms in our gardens by Labor Day and we should be harvesting the first tomatoes sometime around Halloween.

Gardeners have good reasons to be aggrieved this year.

The Diet Backlash Movement

The antidiet revolution has begun. Last month, an article in the Wall Street Journal announced that May 6 was being set aside as International No-Diet Day — "A coalition of health-awareness and pro-fat groups are urging people, 'Speak out! Have a picnic! Smash your bathroom scale!'"

Events were scheduled across North America as rebel leaders, in the words of one spokesperson, "challenged society to stop judging them by the pound." Bagels with full-fat cream cheese and peanut butter were served in Toronto. Seattle celebrated the occasion with a bathroom scale-smashing event. In St. Paul, a fitness shop bought back bathroom scales for $5 and hoped to turned them into a sculpture. They also provided trash cans for fashion magazines.

A protest against the tyranny of the bathroom scale was inevitable and the facts speak for themselves. The average woman is 5 feet 4, weighs 142 pounds and is 44 years old. The average fashion model is 5 feet 9 to six feet, weighs 114 and is about 21.

The truth is out: you can sell skin-tight aerobic outfits to 100 million women, but you can't make them dance. We're not talking about a backlash movement. It's more of a hip, thigh, belly and backlash unmovement. It won't be long before a battle cry is heard throughout the land — "One pizza if by land, two if by sea!" I'm giving serious thought to wearing my "Give me chocolate or give me death" T-shirt on my next trip to town.

How can you tell when antidiet militarism has invaded your own home? The warning signs include the following:

The bathroom scale has been covered with sequins and is being used as a door stop.

Upon closer inspection, the new rose trellises in the garden turn out to be a tread mill and a stationary bike.

Countless checks are being sent to the new charity of choice for your household: the American Snack Food Association.

Menus are centered around potato chips, which have become a main entree.

All clothes with waistbands mysteriously disappear.

Someone will snarl, "What do you mean, 'What are you eating'? I'm eating a chocolate covered, custard-filled bismarck dipped in chocolate milk. Do you want to make something of it?"

The militant announces that she is going on a non-low-fat diet.

Food in general takes on a new element: taste.

A new magnet appears on the refrigerator door: "Bigger is better."

Whenever family members foolishly utter four-letter words such as "diet", "tofu" or "thin", they are ignored completely.

Surprise Weddings

Surprise parties for birthdays and wedding anniversaries have become commonplace events in our country. Now that most people have become used to the idea of walking into their own living rooms and having guests leap from behind draperies, sofas and coffee tables, yelling "Surprise!", we should be aware of a new development — surprise weddings.

Movie stars and other celebrities should be credited with the latest innovation in party-giving. In order to avoid having their weddings overtaken by paparazzi and other party crashers, they are instead whisking their guests off to exotic locations for surprise nuptials. The folks at the Flamingo Hotel in Las Vegas say some couples surprise friends by scheduling weddings to coincide with conventions.

In one surprise wedding scenario, reported in the Wall Street Journal, a couple invited family members on an "engagement cruise". When the ship dropped anchor in St. Thomas, a lunch at the Ritz turned out to be a wedding ceremony. Although the couple was attired in tuxedo and wedding gown, the unsuspecting guests showed up for the "lunch" in wet swimsuits. Surprise. Surprise.

It was the perfect example of an informal wedding. Some weddings are formal — at others you wear your own clothes.

Because surprise weddings in the Caribbean or at Las Vegas might be prohibitive for most household budgets, perhaps we should consider how the surprise element could work in everyday settings.

The grocery store wedding would be an obvious choice.

On the day before the event, phone calls would be made to guests across the country. After being told that your local grocery store is featuring specials on pork and beans, paper plates and dog food, the guests would be unable to resist and they would turn up in droves for the big sale. If they appear reluctant to spend $500 on an airplane ticket, which will enable them to save two dollars on canned goods, employ the double coupon day ruse.

At a grocery store wedding, the cereal aisle could be easily converted into a wedding aisle. The brightly colored boxes of cereal would provide a perfect backdrop for the ceremony. Instead of throwing rice, guests would throw Rice Krispies — countless boxes of them — at the happy couple.

Selecting a day when food samples are available at the store would cut down on catering costs considerably.

"Have you tried the weiner chunks on toothpicks in aisle two? They are absolutely divine!"

If the bride insists on being married in a room filled with flowers, you might be able to lure unsuspecting guests to a greenhouse wedding. Bags of plant fertilizer could easily be transformed into comfortable seating.

While we're being creative, why not hold a wedding in a setting that will appeal to most of the male wedding guests? While the lace, flowers and other trappings of a traditional wedding may not be their idea of excitement, imagine how elated they will be to find themselves at a surprise hardware store wedding. Surrounded by the things they love — power drills, Phillips screwdrivers and duct tape — they might even have a good time.

Surprise weddings — they're not just for celebrities anymore.

The Beetle Makes A Comeback

Imagine being told that you can re-live the thrill of driving one of your first cars. Who would turn down such an opportunity?

Volkswagen AG has announced that the popular Beetle is coming back. The bad news for nostalgia buffs is that the new "bug" has been updated to fit 1990s tastes and technology. According to a newspaper article about the new and improved Beetle, the engine will be moved to the front and the car will have modern accessories such as antilock brakes, airbags and electric windows. The bubble shape will remain, but the car will carry a hefty price tag exceeding $14,0000.

That's not the same car many former Beetle owners can recall owning. Less than 20 years ago, we had three vintage "bugs" parked in our driveway. They had all been purchased with at least 150,000 miles on their odometers and each one perpetuated the myth of automotive immortality.

Although over 22 million Beetles were sold during 60 years of production, making it one of the most popular cars ever sold, many people feared them. Owning a Beetle was an open invitation for ridicule and criticism. Brazen critics referred to the cars as "pregnant rollerskates", "egg beaters" and "tin cans". Their taunts included, "So what do you use to get out of that car? A can opener?"

The naysayers also gave unsolicited, ominous warnings about the car's safety. They went to great lengths describing how a lightweight car with an engine in the back and its passengers would be reduced to a road smear if they would collide head-on with a Mack truck. We, the potential road smears, realized those people were simply jealous because they couldn't find reliable transportation for $200.

Just to be on the safe side, we shied away from Mack trucks.

The Beetles' gas mileage was incredible and their gas tank caps were often covered with cobwebs. We basked in the knowledge that, if we wanted to, we could travel from coast to coast with two or three tanks of gas and an hour's worth of fumes.

It was a safe car. It couldn't go any faster than the average person could think.

We didn't have to worry about parallel parking techniques. The cars could be driven headfirst into any parking place with plenty of room to spare.

On one occasion, while one of our daughters was driving a Beetle to work, the battery dropped from its rusty moorings beneath the backseat and landed on the highway. She managed to coast the car for at least half a mile before she noticed the engine wasn't running.

At another time, while I was unloading groceries from the car, one of my feet crashed through the rust-riddled floor and landed on the driveway. After the gaping hole in the floor was covered with a piece of plywood, the car ran for thousands of more miles.

The VW Beetle was so loveable that Herbie, the "love bug", appeared on the big screen in 1969 and was followed by several sequels. One movie critic described the first film as "a fun-filled Disney romp about a Volkswagen Beetle automobile with a distinct personality and its own ideas of where it wants to go." We never saw similar movies featuring Bucky the Buick or Carlton the Cadillac.

If Volkswagen AG could come up with a way to manufacture $200 Beetles, held together with duct tape and with 150,000 miles already on their odometers, we would be much more willing to experience deja vu.

The Great Spaghetti Sauce Threat

Only a few minutes after take-off, your plane has settled into a comfortable flight pattern. The sky outside the cabin is robin's-egg blue and the passengers seated around you have leaned back in their seats or have opened their books and newspapers. Quite unexpectedly, the captain's voice is heard over the intercom.

"Ladies and gentlemen, don't panic. Our plane has been commandeered by a young woman wielding a quart jar of spaghetti sauce. This is a serious situation. We're talking garlic and herbs."

While this scenario may sound unrealistic, it apparently isn't improbable. Shortly before our daughter's return flight to Rhode Island a few weeks ago, I slipped three quarts of home-canned spaghetti sauce into her carry-on baggage. It was an innocent, motherly gesture and I had no intention of turning her into a tomato terrorist.

At each airport security checkpoint between our home and Providence — Sioux Falls, Minneapolis and Detroit — our daughter and her fiance, who realized by that time he wasn't marrying into a normal family, were subjected to heated questioning about the jars.

"Oh, oh. What's this?"
"Spaghetti sauce."
"Who put it into these jars?"
"My mom."
"Why? Does she do this often?" Fortunately, the interrogators failed to ask the obvious questions: Is your mother a discontent? Does she refer to her close friends as

comrades?

It wasn't the first time my canned goods had been scrutinized by airport security. Five years ago, my husband and I carried two packages aboard a flight to Chicago, when we visited another daughter.

His package, which contained a mantle clock, complete with metal gears and ticking noises, passed through the airport x-ray machines with flying colors. My package, holding three pint jars of pickle relish and three pints of chili sauce, became the cause of great concern. It may have been my imagination, but I was sure I could hear the unsnapping of gun holsters and crackling voices on security walkie-talkies.

I also faced a barrage of questions about the contents of the jars. Evidently, people living in large cities are clueless about home-canning. At one point during the questioning, I was afraid my allegiance to my country might be openly challenged. In spy movies, infiltrators are routinely asked trick questions, such as, "Who won the World Series in 1955?"

For one fleeting moment, I regretted not knowing more about American sports. The World Series. Isn't that baseball?

At each security checkpoint on my daughter's trip, the jars were cautiously removed from the bags and their lids were tapped with ballpoint pens and other instruments. Jars were held up to the light and were tipped in all directions as security personnel looked for possible explosives immersed in the tomato sauce and herbs.

As the jars were poked, prodded and spun around, the possibility was great that their seals could have been broken. From a home-canner's perspective, that would have been a real crime.

A Sow By Any Other Name

If the new terminology from the National Pork Producers Council is adopted, a sow will no longer be a sow. Instead, female pigs will be defined by their mating status.

The five new classifications don't fall trippingly off the tongue: mated breeding female, unmated breeding female, nurse female, prospective breeding female and removed breeding female. In other words, Petunia, Porky Pig's friend, would have been Petunia, The Unmated Breeding Female, a name unlikely to fit on most theatre marquee signs.

I would like to propose a new system for classifying female pigs, which would reflect their basic personalities rather than their breeding status. My assumption is that being viewed simply as a breeding machine would be an affront for females of any species. It would also help if the classifications would rhyme.

For example, a "bow sow" would insist on being formally introduced to any potential suitor.

A "chow sow" would be particularly fond of eating.

In this confusing world, the term "cow sow" would be attached to any female pig having an identity crisis.

A female pig that denies having past relationships with other boars would be called a "disavow sow".

"High brow sows" would demonstrate a higher calling. Their conversations would be sprinkled with words like "enow" and "thou", reflecting their interest in Middle English studies.

A "hausfrau sow" would often exclaim to her offspring, "This place looks like a pigpen!" or "Were you brought up in a barn?"

Female pigs that question everything would be referred to as "how sows".

"Exactly how many litters am I expected to have? How will that happen?"

Their complacent counterparts would be the "kowtow sows", which would also be known as the "allow sows". Any plans Farmer Brown has for them will be perfectly fine.

A "now sow" will simply live for the moment.

Before any boar leads her down the primrose path, a "vow sow" will insist on some sort of commitment.

A "wow sow" would tend be excited about all aspects of her life.

"Hey, this mush tastes great! I love it! Love it! Hey, is this a new trough?"

If the new terminology from the pork producers goes into effect, one well-known proverb will fall by the wayside. "You can't make a silk purse from a sow's ear" would become "You can't make a silk purse from a mated breeding female pig's ear". Something would definitely be lost in the translation.

The New Villains

Hollywood is looking for a few good villains. With the fall of Communism and the rise of political correctness, "bad guys" have changed in the movies.

According to an article in the Wall Street Journal, "Native Americans, once the Western's staple bad guys, have become heroes ('Dances With Wolves') or are off limits. Even remorseless mafia killers now get empathetic treatment (Al Pacino in 'Donnie Brasco'). Protests...have left studios skittish about offending anyone."

The article concludes that the only villains left are dinosaurs ("Jurassic Park"), natural disasters ("Volcano") or aliens ("Men in Black"). Old-fashioned villains have resulted in protests, lawsuits and irate lobbyists.

Villains are alive and well. Movie producers simply haven't known where to look for them. Perhaps they should consider the following movie descriptions:

"Ding Hard" — A band of ruthless terrorists, driving battered vehicles beyond description, roam through parking lots and inflict irreparable damage, in the form of "door dings," upon hapless cars.

"Nightmare on Any Street" — Shameless villains spit on sidewalks, creating precarious paths for unsuspecting pedestrians.

"Nightmare on Any Ball Diamond" — Blockbuster sequel to "Nightmare on Any Street".

"Jack the Picker" — A lone, nose-digging driver singlehandedly ruins the appetites of thousands of other travelers.

"Dial C for Collision" — Drivers using cellular phones create havoc on streets and highways from coast to coast.

"Burger Aliens" — Extraterrestrials take over fast-food restaurants' drive-up windows across the country. In spite of their ability to land on earth undetected, they are unable to master English. As a result, they croak over the intercoms in static-filled voices: "That will (mumble screech mumble) three dollars and (mumble mumble screech) drive forward (mumble screech)."

"Mealbusters" — Indiscriminate telemarketers, most of them with strange accents from other parts of the country, cause countless thousands of nighttime meals to become cold and unpalatable, resulting in widespread public unrest.

"The Incredible Shrinking Woman" — As her unsuspecting victims prepare to enjoy hot fudge sundaes, this heinous creature, disguised as a friend, announces, "No matter how much I eat, I can't gain weight."

"Attack of the Gum People" — Leaving unattractive wads of used chewing gum in their wake, these insidious monsters literally leave their victims stuck to their tracks.

"The Guests Who Wouldn't Leave" — As their numbers multiply during the summer months, these fiends enjoy playing with the minds of their hosts by announcing, "We can only stay a few minutes". Two meals and a quick run to the grocery store later, they have become permanently attached to the victim's living room furniture.

I also doubt whether lobbyists exist for people who put us on hold on the telephone or women who wear stiletto heels and puncture our kitchen flooring. Villains are everywhere.

Trips Out Of This World

According to a 1997 survey conducted by a national leisure travel group, more than 40 percent of Americans "yearn for an out of this world vacation". Specifically, 34 percent of the armchair astronauts said they would like to take a two-week trip aboard a space shuttle and they would be willing to spend about $10,800 for the travel package.

A NASA spokesman, George Diller, thinks that dream may materialize in 10 to 15 years, but he foresees a trip lasting an hour and costing $50,000. Passengers would experience weightlessness for about 15 minutes.

At that hourly rate, many of us would experience creditlessness for an additional seven years.

Before we pack our toothbrushes, sell everything we own and head for the Kennedy Space Center, it might be wise to consider the pros and cons of such a trip. For starters, given our weight-conscious society, it might be worth $50,000 to be able to mention in casual conversations that we weigh zero pounds.

A trip into space would change the dynamics of traveling with small children. There would be no cries of "I can't see anything from the backseat" because the passing landscape would be minimal. We wouldn't be subjected to the universal complaint, "Hey, we passed a McDonald's!"

Our trips wouldn't run the risk of being spoiled by rain, unseasonable temperatures, earthquakes, hurricanes, tornadoes or speeding tickets.

We would be unable to mail postcards back home

to friends and relatives ("Having a great time. Be back in an hour.") and spacesuits would solve the problem about which clothes to pack.

Travelers who insist on getting out of a vehicle every 100 miles to stretch their legs would be able to do so — but only once. After their first steps into outer space they would simply be referred to as "the satellites".

We wouldn't need extra spending money for countless souvenir stands along the way. We would be unable to fill our suitcases for the trip home with bumper stickers, motel soaps or small garments reading, "My mom and dad traveled to outer space and all I got was this lousy T-shirt."

Reaching zero gravity in space creates other advantages. Astronauts have found that blood that normally settles in the legs is allowed to drift upward. As a result, their legs become thinner and their chests expand by two to three inches. Because of the freer blood circulation, their faces fill out and wrinkles disappear.

What person in his or her right mind would turn down those possibilities? Hello, outer space and better bodies. Goodbye, thunder thighs and wrinkles.

On the other hand, landing back on earth would leave a space traveler wobbly-kneed, light-headed and slightly disoriented. But who doesn't feel that way after any vacation?

Our Worst Fears

According to a scientific poll on fear, conducted recently by USA Weekend, Americans are finding plenty of reasons to lose sleep. The highest ranked fears, affecting at least 36 percent of us, include being in a car crash, having cancer, inadequate Social Security, not enough money for retirement and food poisoning from meat.

I must belong to the other 64 percent because most of my fears are related to mundane, everyday events. For instance, I don't lie awake nights worrying about Social Security coverage, but the fear of having my high school diploma recalled after 37 years because I missed one semester of physical education is enough to put me over the edge.

The fears gleaned by the pollsters were too big and too grand for most of us. In real life, fears are much more personal than worrying about electromagnetic fields (16 percent according to the poll) or natural disasters (25 percent).

For example, there's the fear of being told you're too old to ride on a roller coaster. Other garden variety fears would include:

Being weighed at the doctor's office.

Going to the dentist's office for an estimate.

Arriving at the grocery store and discovering you left your shopping list on the kitchen counter.

Being told that you look and act exactly like your mother.

Going through an entire day with lipstick or a chunk of food stuck to your front teeth.

Being attacked by bees, mosquitoes or rabid squirrels.

Having drop-in visitors during dinner time.

Hearing the phone ring during the middle of the night.

Being under 50 and having a 17-year-old salesclerk ask if you want a senior citizen's discount.

Being told that your car or a favorite major appliance is dead.

Being asked to appear on a daytime TV talk show with a miscontent who wishes to discuss your faults.

Having your golf scores announced on ESPN.

Blowing up a balloon and having it explode in your face.

Being chosen as a poster child for an eating disorders group.

Having a physical examination and hearing the doctor say, "Oh, oh."

Being told that you will have to become a surrogate mother and give birth to your own grandchildren.

Being advised that you have developed a life-threatening allergy to chocolate.

These fears may not appear on the USA Weekend survey, but they are nevertheless real.

Let's Export Baseball Caps

Hat problems are brimming on both sides of the Atlantic Ocean. In what could prove to be an amazing trade-off, one country's problem could be another country's solution.

England needs more hats. Specifically, it needs replacements for the 18-inch-tall bearskin hats worn by elite military regiments since the 1815 British victory over Napoleon's forces at Waterloo. The hats are worn for ceremonial duties and by the soldiers chosen to guard royal residences and the Tower of London.

According to an Associated Press story, the old, worn out, Canadian bearskin hats need to be replaced by fake furs. Past attempts to use synthetic bearskin have ended in disaster. When it rained, "the hats became rather bedraggled — like a bad hair day", noted one military spokesman.

He added, "They were also subject to static electricity, which was rather embarrassing when they passed under electricity pylons." Evidently, the country didn't want to be represented by soldiers resembling fight manager Don King.

On this side of the big pond, we have an overabundance of headwear, notably baseball caps. The caps multiply at a greater rate than factories can possibly be manufacturing them. They are found in restaurants, on the streets and at weddings and other social events. The caps appear to be permanently welded to their wearers' heads and they are no longer removed inside buildings or in the presence of women.

I suspect that whenever two caps are stored in the

same closet overnight, they reproduce with reckless abandon. A baseball cap casually thrown into the backseat of a car becomes a row of caps in the car's back window.

"Honey, don't look now, but when we left Omaha a few hours ago, weren't there only three caps in the backseat?"

In addition to breaking every etiquette rule about the wearing of hats, baseball caps have created physical side-effects. Increasing numbers of American men are experiencing white foreheads and permanent creases or dents in their hair, commonly referred to as Cap Head. Their misshapen hairlines are not unlike the impressions created by anvils on soft metals.

If we were to ship a small fraction of our country's baseball caps — perhaps two or three million — to the British soldiers, two problems could be solved at the same time. Of course, the recipients would run the risk of assuming a baseball cap attitude.

Buckingham Palace guards are required to stand at rigid attention without flinching a muscle. They have to stand poker-faced while tourists test their mettle, trying to make them talk or even smile.

All of that rigidity might vanish if the guards would opt for the headgear originally worn on our baseball diamonds. Without meaning to, they might feel compelled to spit on the ground, chew juicy wads of tobacco, scratch themselves in embarrassing places or demand higher wages.

The baseball caps may not be the perfect solution, but I'm sure the Canadian bears would approve.

A Guide To Home Weddings

When our second daughter called us last March to tell us about her engagement, we were elated. Seconds later, when she announced that she would like to be married in our house in October, we were calm and unshaken.

After all, October was seven months, two seasons and light years away. During that time a wayward satellite could make a direct hit on our house or a tornado could level the house and negate the need to clean closets. In the event that a natural disaster would fail to do its work, we could always move without giving the post office a forwarding address. Anything can happen in seven months.

Last week, when it became fairly obvious that the wedding would take place, I did something out of character — I checked out Martha Stewart's wedding book at the public library. The chapter titled "Home Weddings" would surely solve all of my problems.

After shoving aside the accumulated clutter on my kitchen counter, I found space to open the book. The chapter on home weddings showed homes bearing no resemblance to our own. Gardens were overflowing with flowers and herbs, lawns were fastidiously manicured and beautiful people lounged on Adirondack chairs. Even the horse stables shown in the photos were neater and more tastefully decorated than our living room on a good day.

With the realization that there can only be one Martha Stewart, I have come up with a five-word solution that will give any daughter's home wedding the illusion of being well organized and elegant — keep them in the dark.

No wedding guest should be allowed on your property until the sun has set completely. During daylight-saving time this might mean that a couple wouldn't exchange vows until nearly midnight. On the other hand, few newlyweds would turn down the opportunity to spend their wedding night surrounded by friends, neighbors and relatives.

All of the light bulbs in the house should be replaced with weaker 10-watt bulbs and candles. In better restaurants this is called ambience. Dim lighting will also make the food look more appetizing. With the proper lighting a dish of blackberry jam will be easily mistaken for the most expensive caviar. It will also taste better.

After dark the sun won't be highlighting window streaks or the dirt lines left behind on the panes by last winter's snowdrifts.

Specify on the wedding invitations that guests should wear neither black ties nor dark formal wear, but rather dust-colored clothing. This will eliminate the need to dust or vacuum, both thankless tasks, before the big day.

Loosen the bulbs in outdoor light fixtures. Guests will be less likely to wander into the tomato patch, well past its prime, or onto the lawn, which resembles a green, bad hair day.

Our daughter's wedding will take place October 25, and I can't be sure during that time of year whether our lawn will be mercifully obliterated with leaves or whether it will look like a winter scene out of "Dr. Zhivago". I do know, however, that if a guest notices one of our many cobwebs in the faint candlelight, I will quickly explain that it's only six days until Halloween. The cobwebs are intentional.

Mice Invasions

According to d-CON, the vermin poison people, October is National Rodent Prevention Month. Not coincidentally, this is also the time of year when millions of mice invade houses and garages.

Mice invasions are rarely brought up in polite conversations, and they are akin to other unmentionable topics such as body odor, halitosis, loose dentures and creeping underwear. We all know these problems exist but we'll never admit to dealing with them.

Except for the discreet stockpiling of mouse traps and poisons in our stores, there are no other indications that our country is gearing up for an annual, all-out war against mice. Salesclerks silently slide the weapons over their scanners and avoid saying the obvious, "Aha! I can see by your purchases that your house is infested with mice."

Unwritten rules govern mouse extermination protocol. Never have mousetraps in clear sight when you're entertaining guests or when you're showing the house to prospective buyers. Insist that family members tread lightly around the house or that they wear steel-tipped shoes. For a reason which will be given later, wear short hair.

In 1889, Ralph Waldo Emerson noted, "If a man can...make a better mouse-trap than his neighbor...the world will make a beaten path to his door." In spite of poisoned bait, spring-action traps, glue traps and live traps, which claim to be more humane, the world is still waiting.

Poisoned bait causes mice to die between walls. If

you don't want to tear out perfectly good sheetrock, rip out insulation and grope around for something you don't really want to find, memories of the mice may linger for as long as two weeks. Your only alternative is to find a good sale on room sprays.

Spring-action traps are much like dishwashers. No one thinks twice about loading them, but nobody wants to empty them.

Glue traps resemble "Twister", the popular floor game from the 1960s. If contact cement would have been applied to the plastic playing field and players would have assumed permanent pretzel positions, you have a fairly good idea of what the mice go through with glue traps.

Live traps are often clear plastic boxes with one-way trap doors. Mice are enticed into the boxes with cheese chunks or peanut butter globs but they are unable to escape. The live traps are designed so that homeowners will be able to release the animals unharmed in the outside world. The possibility of tilting the trap at the wrong angle and having the one-way trapdoor become unhinged, which would allow the mouse to run up your arm, around your neck and down your leg, isn't addressed in the trap's instructions.

Twenty years ago, when large, fuzzy hair permanents were the rage, our family lived in a 100-year-old farmhouse. Early one morning, while the sky was still pitch-black and two hours before I had to leave for a meeting in Minneapolis, I awoke to the realization that my scalp was being scratched. As my eyes tried to adjust to my surroundings, it became quite clear that I wasn't doing the scratching and neither was my husband.

A mouse had become entangled in my hair. With a shriek of terror, I sat up and swatted the top of my head. Once. Twice. Three times. A thunk was finally heard against a nearby wall and tiny mice feet scampered off to another part of the house.

My hair was shampooed and reshampooed for the next hour, but nothing could erase the image of sitting at a meeting in Minneapolis and having tiny, pink baby mice falling from my head and onto the conference table.

That's why it's important to wear short hair during National Rodent Prevention Month.

The New, Improved $50 Bill

In a world where "new and improved" laundry detergents, anti-perspirants and countless other products are introduced on a daily basis, the U.S. Treasury has joined the action. We now have a new and improved $50 note, following the introduction of a new and improved $100 note in 1996.

I first learned of the new $50 bill in a full-color brochure, printed by the U.S. Treasury Department and enclosed with my last bank statement. The slick brochure undoubtedly marks the first time that any government has spent millions of dollars to explain a piece of paper worth $50.

Unfortunately, few people will notice the changes. As we head into a moneyless society, electronic banking and its progeny — money cards, credit cards and purchases made through personal computers — are replacing paper currency. The only times Americans need real money is when they are dealing in illegal transactions, paying ransom money or they are slipping a few bills into graduation or wedding cards.

The main changes in the new and improved $50 bill feature a larger, off-center portrait of Ulysses S. Grant, a watermark portrait in the paper, color-shifting ink, non-replicable fine-line printing and a large 50 on the note's back for the visually impaired.

Although the changes are ostensibly for security reasons, the brochure includes so many unnecessary details that it could serve as a how-to manual for counterfeiter wannabes. For example, should we know that the words, "United States of America", are finely printed in Grant's collar?

The new notes also have a plastic, security thread imbedded in the paper, a feature first introduced in 1990. The invisible thread glows a bright yellow when held under an ultraviolet light. Most of the stores I frequent don't bother with universal price codes. How will they find the wherewithal to use ultraviolet lights at their checkout counters?

Nowhere in the brochure is mention made of public input in the redesigning of the new $50 note. The Treasury Department's changes may be fine and dandy and they may make our world a safer place, but John or Jane Q. Public might have offered the following suggestions:

Adhesives imbedded in the paper would make it less easy to part with what real money we do have.

Blank spaces should be provided for last minute grocery lists or personalized notes such as, "MF desires new tuna fish casserole recipes. Call 555-5555 and ask for Tootie."

Spending money could be more fun if a "Where's Waldo?" game would appear on the note.

Above all, a printed guarantee should be on the bill, regardless of its denomination, assuring the consumer that the note will always be worth its face value.

Eating Becomes An Art

Art, like beauty, is no longer in the eye of the beholder. Rather, it's in the eye of the table napkin holder.

Ming-Wei Lee's recent performance-art exhibit in a New York City gallery featured him merely eating dinner, in private, with a new guest each night. Plate art has suddenly been elevated to great art.

"Both of us are performing," the artist noted. "Both of us are participating. The food acts as a medium for conversation. For me, art is about process."

The exhibit threw a new light on an old bromide — "I don't know anything about art, but I know what I like" is now "I don't know anything about art, but I know what I like to eat." If Lee's new art form catches on, we can expect to be surrounded by artists described as low-fat, haute cuisine or vegetarian.

I wonder what kinds of comments art critics and casual observers were expected to make as they watched two people eating a meal. After all, a trip to a downtown gallery in New York City, which would certainly involve more than a walk around the block, requires more than a simple, "Gee, that food looks good."

Instead, someone might note, "Look at the perfect symmetry of those meatballs", to which another art patron would respond, "Do you sense the angry mood of that crease in the tablecloth?"

In addition to noting the spatial relationship of the water glass to the forks and knives, another observer might remark, "Watching the syncopated rhythm as they chew their pasta leaves me absolutely breathless!" Only so much can be said about watching two people as they sit down and devour a meal in an art gallery.

Of course, Lee's performance-art exhibit wasn't the first connection between food and art. L.S. Lowry once remarked, "Art? Art? All the art in the world isn't worth a good meat and potato pie." Had he lived to see Lee's exhibit, Ralph Waldo Emerson wouldn't have stopped with his observation, "Art is a jealous mistress." He might have added, "It is also a well-set table."

Instead of saying, "If that's art, I'm a Hottentot", President Harry S. Truman might have noted, "If that's art, I'm a hotdish."

For the sake of those unable to attend Lee's show in New York City, similar performance-art tableaus will be offered at my home during the next few weeks. For a nominal fee, participants will be able to enjoy three variations of Lee's new art form: "Two People Weather-stripping the Windows", "Two People Raking Leaves" and "Two People Staining House Siding." We will all benefit from the process, as Lee calls it.

If the three exhibits prove to be successful, I might even change my opinions about performance-art.

Going Nowhere For $80,000

There's hope for parents of noncommunicative teenagers. Ever since the word teenager was first coined, certain parents have worried that their offspring will never find a meaningful place in society or a sense of direction. The following conversation often occurs in their homes:

"You're back. Where did you go?"
"Nowhere."
"What did you do?"
"Nothing."

Those young people may be perfect candidates for the Concorde plane trips to nowhere which will soon be departing from Kennedy Airport in New York. The only drawback to the trips is that there may be some hard work involved.

The Wall Street Journal reported, "Air France has just introduced group Concorde flights with no destination, which it hopes to sell as the ultimate reward for hard-working corporate employees. The itinerary is simple. As many as 100 passengers board the Concorde at Kennedy, hurtle over the Atlantic, then turn around and fly back. The entire journey takes less than two hours and costs $80,000 for the planeload."

A short trip to nowhere is now a reality.

So far, Air France has had no takers for the trips that allow for little else than a takeoff and a landing. When it comes to incentives, employers seem to think they could do a lot more for $800 a person. With even the cost of going up going up, they fail to see the benefits of going nowhere fast.

Taking a two-hour trip with no destination would allow passengers to return home before they experience indigestion from the mystery meat included in the plane meal.

There would be no suitcases to pack or lug around and dirty laundry at the end of the trip wouldn't be a problem.

The trip would end before you would have time to misplace your billfold, passport or plane tickets.

You wouldn't have to worry about finding your car in a 2,000-acre airport parking lot upon your return. You could leave your car idling in the loading zone.

You wouldn't have to worry about having a bad plane seat on the way home.

No one would expect you to keep in touch with scenic postcards from some exotic port of call.

Author Robert Louis Stevenson would have also been a perfect candidate for the incentive travel plan offered by Air France. In 1879 he wrote, "For my part, I travel not to go anywhere, but to go. I travel for travel's sake. The great affair is to move."

Stevenson, who lived at least a century before his time, also noted, "There's nothing under Heav'n so blue that's fairly worth the travelling to."

He would have relished the Concorde flight to nowhere.

A Pedicurist For Cows

A pedicurist in Michigan is udderly pleased with his change in clients. According to the Associated Press, Jim Rondy, a 26-year-old from Fowler, Michigan, reports that he makes more than $100,000 a year working exclusively on the hooves of milk cows.

Rondy tends cows at 90 farms, making $10 a head trimming hooves and removing unsightly mud and manure. Although removing barnyard waste may not sound like everybody's idea of an ideal job or a good time, the Michigan pedicurist undoubtedly realizes some definite advantages in his work.

Without fearing repercussions, he can honestly say that at least one of his clients is definitely Bossy.

He doesn't have to worry about making small talk with his pedicurees. There's no need to remember the names of a client's husbands or children because those facts aren't important to a cow either. In addition, when a client shows up for an appointment wearing only a cowbell and a numbered ear-tag, he isn't required to say something nice about her outfit.

He doesn't have to fear offending his clients with off-the-wall humor, such as "Have you herd this?" or "Let's just relax and shoot the bull." When he's kicked in the head by a belligerent customer, he feels free to ask, "What's the deal, honey? Were you brought up in a barn?"

He doesn't expect to be tipped by his customers, so there are no disappointments about gratuities.

Cows are far superior to human clients. Author George Eliot once noted, "Animals are such agreeable friends; they ask no questions and pass no criticisms."

If those advantages and the possibility of earning $100,000 a year appeal to you, perhaps you should consider turning tail and becoming a cow pedicurist.

However, there are some obvious pitfalls to avoid as you drive from farm to farm looking for work:

Don't apply for the job wearing a pink smock, open-toed spiked heels or glitter in your hair.

Don't mention that you want to remove "doodoo" from the cows' hooves.

Don't expect cooperation if you attempt to do a pedicure on a cow called "El Toro".

Trade in your tray of nail polishes, cotton balls and emery boards for a heavy-duty chisel. Forget how smashing Cow Number Thirty-three would look if her hooves were covered with "Fire Engine Red."

When being interviewed by a prospective employer, don't mention that you're a vegetarian or that you think cows are cute.

Above all, watch your step. If you're hired and your new employer tells you to be on the lookout for cowpies, he's not talking lunch.

Effects Of El Nino

Kin Hubbard once observed, "Don't knock the weather; nine-tenths of people couldn't start a conversation if it didn't change once in a while." With the event of El Nino, the water warming phenomenon in the Pacific Ocean, we nine-tenths have plenty of conversation starters.

We are no longer content to pass along casual yet mundane comments about the weather — "Hot enough for you?"or "That was really a gully washer last night."

Those nine-tenths of us, who once endured TV weather forecasts because we didn't want to miss the sports scores that followed, now sound like bona fide meteorologists. We can readily repeat the predictions: high winds, pounding surf and sheets of rain for most of California, a warmer and drier Northwest, snow deprivation for parts of the Rockies and the Great Plains, wetter and colder conditions for Florida and the Gulf Coast, and a milder winter for the Atlantic Coast and the Northeast.

Weather phrases, such as "east-west flows of trade winds" and "infrared satellite images" have permeated our everyday language. The fervor over El Nino has been punctuated, both figuratively and literally, with journalists scrambling to locate the squiggly lines, the tildes, to place over n's in their news stories.

On the bright side, TV weather segments have become mini-geography lessons and we are now able to locate Denver,Acapulco and the Pacific Ocean with fair accuracy on world maps.

El Nino is also shaping up as the perfect scapegoat

for any unusual event. When Denver and certain points eastward were buried under several feet of snow this winter, people were quick to blame the water warming in the Pacific. That blame, that nino pointing, will undoubtedly be transferred to all aspects of our lives.

Is you car using more oil lately? Blame El Nino. Are your grades dropping in school? Blame El Nino. Before this winter ends, we will be using the water warming as an excuse for everything from collapsed cakes in ovens to why we can't seem to shed those extra twenty pounds.

As El Nino becomes an everyday expression, we can also expect it to influence new words in our vocabulary. In the same way that the noun "microwave" became a verb, El Nino may also assume other forms. (While it's perfectly all right to offer, "Let me microwave that popcorn for you", we never say "I'm going to oven the turkey" or "Let's refrigerator the leftovers").

Office workers, watching a colleague receive a pink slip, will comment, "It looks like George is being ninoed."

We can expect to hear, "Sorry to nino your day, Sir, but you were speeding back there."

The good news is that El Ninos have been around for centuries. In fact, we've had 13 since 1950. There will always be another nino to blame and to talk about.

The Cookie Baking Contest

Except for a close encounter with a cookie terrorist, one of my lifelong fantasies came true last weekend. I had been asked to judge a cookie-baking contest at a local discount store and life seemed fairly perfect when I was told that my work would involve judging plattersful of cookies on the basis of appearance, texture and "general yumminess".

While other people's fantasies may involve being asked to pilot a 747 during an emergency landing or receiving a trivia question phone call from Regis Philbin and Kathie Lee Gifford, most of my daydreams have had something to do with food. Food, particularly cookies, has been responsible for both my destiny and my density.

Unlike actress Sophia Loren, who once noted, "All you see, I owe to spaghetti", I would have to admit, "All you see, I owe to cookies."

When I arrived at the contest table in the store, appropriately located between racks of ladies' stretch slacks and over-sized sweaters, I could understand the thrill experienced by pilgrims as they approach Mecca. Eight paper plates, each covered with one dozen taste-tantalizing cookies, baked with loving hands by the best home-bakers in the area, were awaiting the final decisions.

After doing some quick mental calculations and after meeting the only other judge, the store manager with a flat, firm stomach, I guess-timated that my share of the bounty could be at least 50 cookies. As the manager and I filled in the score sheets before the actual testing, a young boy, perhaps 11 or 12 years old, approached the table.

I instantly sensed trouble when he asked, "Are those cookies for sale?" The interloper looked as if he was capable of eating his own weight in cookies.

"No, they aren't," replied the manager. "They're here for a contest." They boy took one step backward, and then lunged forward quite unexpectedly, his outreached hand within an inch of plate number seven, which was piled high with chocolate chip and black walnut cookies.

For one fleeting second I considered knocking the cookie terrorist senseless to the floor with my bulky, over-the-shoulder purse. After all, territorial rights were definitely an issue.

Before I had the opportunity to send the lad spiraling with 20 pounds of credit cards and loose change, the manager intervened and calmly explained, "These cookies are not for sale. They're not free. They're contest cookies." The boy, suddenly aware of his mistake, backed off and disappeared behind a display of men's boxer shorts.

Equipped with clipboards and newly sharpened pencils, the other judge and I decided to start our contest sampling from opposite ends of the table. By the time we had reached the middle of the table, it became clear that our approaches to taste-testing differed considerably. While he had been taking one bite from each plate, I had been devouring entire cookies by the mouthful. By the time I had eaten at least six cookies from plates one, two and three, my blood-sugar level had reached a record-breaking high and my ears were buzzing.

When the final winners were determined, a dozen cookies later, I was succumbing to a series of out-of-the-body experiences and I could only mumble incoherently. My cookie-judging fantasy hadn't included an overdose of chocolate chips, chocolate frosting and sugar sprinkles.

David Sarnoff must have been thinking about cookie contests when he told Esquire magazine, "Competition brings out the best in products and the worst in people."

Computerized Grave Markers

Like it or not, computers have already invaded most aspects of our lives. If a company in Lebanon, Ohio, has its way, computers will also take over our final resting places.

According to Time magazine, Leif Technologies is selling grave markers called "computerized, visual eulogy systems". Flush-mounted screens in the $4,000 markers will have enough memory to hold up to 250 pages of photos, life stories and last words. Having the last word is evidently the last word in computer technology.

In William Shakespeare's "Richard II", a character intoned, "Let's talk of graves." Times have changed since the bard's day — it now appears that our graves will do the talking for us.

If nothing else, the computerized markers will give new meaning to the expression, "Rest in Peace." The "R.I.P." engravings, long taken for granite, will eventually stand for "Rest in Programming."

The memory capacity of the stone's chip would have solved one problem faced by a former politician in Dayton, Ohio. His epitaph reads: "Here, reader, turn your weeping eyes, My fate a useful moral teaches; The hole in which my body lies would not contain one-half my speeches." The 250-page memory might have solved his dilemma about having too many words and not enough space.

Now that Leif Technologies' plans for remarkable markers are more or less etched in stone, we can expect to see new problems. For example, knowing the difference between hardware and software was difficult enough. Now we will be expected to know everything about tombwear.

The Ohio company is also asking buyers to choose between extended life batteries, to keep the computer screens running, or eternal solar power cells. Both power sources have their drawbacks. Extended life batteries, a definite misnomer, would require a responsible survivor to change them once in a while. That's a dismal prospect if your children had a tendency to put off doing homework or often forgot to feed the dog.

On the other hand, your screen's memory could be erased completely if your only power source was the sun and your last real estate purchase was exposed to countless days of overcast skies.

There's also the prospect that someone will come up with the idea of having not only visual eulogies, but also musical enhancements. Are we prepared to spend centuries next to a recording of some guy singing "Tie a Yellow Ribbon 'Round the Old Oak Tree" or the theme music from "Take This Job and Shove It"? Do we really want to be exposed to Muzak well into the next millennium?

The idea of having a computerized tombstone is definitely a grave matter.

The Advantages Of Snail Mail

Some traditions are hard to break. Most U.S. consumers would rather have their correspondence and bills sent by "snail mail" than by electronic mail. That's the finding of Bitney Bowes, the company that commissioned a survey of 1,300 adults.

The survey revealed that 88.5 percent of Americans prefer getting bills via first-class mail, 81.2 percent want to have personal correspondence delivered by a letter carrier, and 71.8 percent want their business correspondence hand-delivered. According to an Associated Press article about the respondents, "They believe first-class mail is the most secure and least intrusive way to get mail."

It would be difficult to imagine a world without letters that have been signed, sealed and delivered. There's a special delight in receiving an envelope that has been run over someone's tongue at least twice and has been lovingly handled by dozens of postal workers.

A computerized mail system would undermine the ordinary patterns of our lives, particularly the lives of us who live on rural mail delivery routes. I would miss pushing up the little red flag on the mailbox to indicate I have outgoing mail or chatting with the mail carrier about the weather, the roads and the ills of the world.

Without mail deliveries, certain residents of the Upper Midwest would have fewer reasons to go outside during the six or seven months of winter. We wouldn't be able to look into the jaws of death or have our lives flash before our eyes as we leap over snowdrifts, slip across patches of ice and trip over shovels fast-frozen into snowbanks as we retrieve our daily allotments of junk mail.

We wouldn't be able to savor unopened envelopes in our hands as we check out return addresses and postmarks and wonder what the letters inside will reveal. Computers can't be held up to the light to see what's inside. There would be no turning over a greeting card and asking the question that has troubled mankind for decades, "Did they care enough to send the very best?"

Electronic mail would reduce possibilities for inflicting parental guilt.

"Dear Son: I broke my hip on the way out to the mailbox yesterday, but thank you for the postcard from your winter break in Florida, anyway."

E-mail, as it's known in computer circles, would also deprive us of the satisfaction of writing scathing letters to persons who have wronged us, and never mailing them. Abraham Lincoln, an expert on this matter, once told a colleague, "You have freed your mind on the subject, and that is all that is necessary. Tear it up. You never want to send such letters; I never do."

Romanticism would fall by the wayside. George Bernard Shaw noted, "The ideal love affair is one conducted by post." In cases of unrequited love, tears splashing against a computer screen wouldn't have the effect of tears mixing with the ink on a "Dear John" letter.

Electronic mail, which allows for split-second financial transactions, would eliminate the well-worn excuse, "The check is in the mail."

Rudyard Kipling would have been the greatest proponent of snail mail. In "The Shut-Eye Sentry" he wrote, "Give 'im a letter — Can't do no better."

Realism And Barbie Dolls

In Oscar Wilde's story, "The Picture of Dorian Gray", a man's portrait reflects his decadence, even though the man appears quite normal in person. What Wilde did for decadence Mattel Inc. is now doing with its Barbie doll and the aging process.

While female baby boomers may not care to think about it, their appearances change and their cargoes shift as they approach mid-life. At the toy industry's annual trade fair in January, a 38-year-old Barbie will be introduced with a wider waist, a decreased chestline, less makeup and a closed mouth.

Although a Mattel spokesman told the Wall Street Journal that the new look is a reflection of changing times and tastes, any middle-ager would suspect that Barbie's closed mouth conceals partial-denture work done by Ken the Dentist.

It's very possible that in 10 or 20 years, small girls will tear open boxes under their Christmas trees, only to discover they own Grandma Barbies. A storybook enclosed with the doll will explain how the once sparkling-eyed blonde actually eloped with Ken in 1977 and that they had three children after they settled down in relative obscurity in a small town in the Midwest.

The Mattel spokesman noted, "Children today clamor for greater realism."

"Mattel is already looking ahead to new variations on a 38-year-old theme," added the Wall Street Journal.

If this Mattel plan to have a doll which reflects its past owners follows through, baby boomers will have more than their share of reflective realism. Along with Cellulite Barbie, which will be attached to a tiny liposuction machine, the next step will include the 20-Year High School Reunion Barbie, who will look like she has starved for four weeks.

Those models will be followed by Varicose Barbie, which will be accessorized with support stockings and sensible shoes, and Facelift Barbie, capable of having wrinkle lines drawn on her face and then wiped off.

Estrogen Barbie, also known as Hot Flash Barbie, will come fully equipped with a miniature electric blanket, a portable fan and a tiny furnace thermostat which can be attached to a wall of her Dream Castle.

The Graying Hair Barbie ("Watch her hair color turn from gray to blue to red!") will lead the way for Retired Barbie ("Help Barbie spend her $200 a month!") and Snow Bird Barbie, who will be permanently attached to the front seat of a motor home.

Years from now, we will remember how Barbie's transformation began with a widened waistline and a diminished chest in 1998. Not only will art imitate life, but so will Barbie dolls.

Salts, Fats And Sugar: Back To The Basics

If a recent survey is any indication, a record number of Americans will be diving into hot buttered rum, frothy eggnog, sugar cookies and mounds of salt during the upcoming holidays.

In its annual survey of 2,500 consumers nationwide, Yankelovich Partners, a research company based in Norwalk, Connecticut, found that interest in nutrition has dropped from 40 percent to 36 percent during the past three years. The survey also showed that weight concerns have dropped from 37 percent to 29 percent in less than that time.

Roughly translated, that means that 71 percent of us are returning to the basics that made this country great: fat, sugar and salt. The scales were tipped in more than one way when a recent Harvard study suggested that trans-fats, the result of transforming oils into solid or semi-solid margarine, increase the risk of a heart attack 53 percent more than do bacon drippings, lard, butter and real cheese.

Writing in Newsday, Robert Reno asked, "How badly have Americans been taken to the cleaners in the past 40 years, not just by charlatans marketing fad diets and miracle cures, but by mainstream dietary wise men peddling advice that turns out to be either worthless or harmful?"

This might explain why so many Americans are giving up on so-called healthy diets. They are literally fed up with food study reversals. If these reversals continue, we may expect to hear the following revelations in the not too distant future:

"It has been noted that smokers exhibit a higher resistance to harsh weather than do non-smokers. After years of having smokers in shirtsleeves banished to alleyways and sidewalks outside offices and businesses in all sorts of weather — rain, sleet, hail and snow — it has been determined that the advantages of smoking far outweigh its disadvantages. Smokers also exhibit more outgoing personalities, as evidenced by their willingness to share their spaces and to huddle closely with complete strangers."

"The dangers of excessive coffee drinking are debunked in a new study, which shows that people who drink 15-20 cups of coffee a day are more likely to understand the intricacies of indoor plumbing systems. They are also more familiar with the exact locations of restroom facilities along interstate and secondary highways between work and home. They may be more agitated, but they are also more knowledgeable."

"Consumers of potato chips exhibit better thumb-forefinger dexterity than do non-chip eaters. Potato chip aficionados have demonstrated an uncanny ability to seize objects of varying shapes and sizes within a short time."

"The advantages of eating excessive amounts of salt were outlined in a new study today. Salt eaters are less likely to pass out during extremely hot weather and they require very few stops during extended car trips because of their superior fluid retention."

"It has been confirmed that heavy consumers of cholesterol have more body mass, which enables them to survive longer on deserted islands following shipwrecks."

"In light of the fact that all elements on earth are divided into three categories — animals, vegetables and minerals — it has been determined by the Surgeon General that chocolate is indeed a vegetable, not unlike broccoli and green beans."

Perhaps the best health advice of all came from Mark Twain, who wrote, "Part of the secret of success in life is to eat what you like and let the food fight it out inside." According to the survey, 71 percent of us will carry his advice into the new year.

New Year's Resolutions

Do you need other reasons to celebrate this holiday season? According to a nationally distributed calendar of events, December 31 has been set aside for three noble causes.

A group called the Long Haul Committee calls that day "You're All Done Day" and celebrants are urged to honor themselves for all they have accomplished during the past year. In my particular case, that should take about two minutes.

December 31 is also National Make Up Your Mind Day and No Resolution Day, sponsored by people who make it a point not to make New Year's resolutions. Although these two causes seem contradictory, there's a strong possibility that most of us will follow the second, more traveled path.

No Resolution Day fits in nicely with the findings of a survey of 2,500 consumers by Yankelovich Partners, a research company based in Connecticut. Most respondents noted that their primary goal for the new year is "to have fun". Fun doesn't imply a nationwide willingness to give up tasty food, long hours in front of the television or the freedom to wear the same socks two days in a row. The survey indicates that most of us are happy with the status quo.

The main trouble with New Year's resolutions is that they are destined for failure. If they are made, they should be more obtainable. For example, rather than pledging to eat only lettuce, soybean curd and celery for the rest of our lives, an unrealistic goal, we should decide that we will only eat to excess while we're awake.

Instead of promising ourselves to brush and floss our teeth after every meal, we will be content to settle with two or three times a day. Brushing after every meal is an unattainable goal because few of us would have the time to brush our teeth eight times a day.

Anyone concerned with the appearance of a home should vow to wash the windows at the onset of every month with 32 days.

The oil should be changed in our cars at least once during the upcoming year.

It's safe to pledge that we will pay our income taxes on or before April 15.

Our 1997 Christmas cards will be mailed and the outside Christmas lights will be taken down before the Fourth of July.

We should promise ourselves that we won't try to break any world record by giving birth to octuplets this year.

In keeping with our nation's desire to have more fun this year, we will ignore the advice of traditional diet and exercise gurus and we will begin calling our midday meal "funch".

Our fitness guru will be Robert Maynard Hutchins, who once wrote, "Whenever I feel like exercise, I lie down until the feeling passes."

The late humorist Fred Allen also knew about obtainable resolutions and the importance of having fun. He observed, "I like long walks, especially when they are taken by people who annoy me."

Clearly, walking and other New Year's resolutions should be taken in stride.

Leona Sells Her House

Leona Helmsley's house in Paradise Valley, Arizona, isn't your typical three-bedroom rambler in the suburbs. The New York real estate magnate, who served 18 months in prison for tax evasion after allegedly saying "only the little people pay taxes," is asking $25 million for her secluded 20,000-square-foot home.

According to a recent newspaper story, that's five times the price for other luxury homes in the area and $19 million more than what she paid for the property 10 years ago. The 10-acre estate includes a 36-foot waterfall that cascades into a lagoon pool and a bathroom with 24-karat gold faucets. The real estate ad also lists 12 bathrooms, elevators, staff quarters and three pools, including an Olympic-sized pool with an underwater sound system.

Twenty-five million sounds like a lot of money to spend in order to hear the poorer neighbors with $5 million homes sigh, "There goes the neighborhood." If most of us were able to raise the $25 million — perhaps by telling the FBI our grandparents had been kidnapped and we needed the money fast —it's highly improbable we would have enough money to fill the pools with water or pay for a riding lawn mower.

We would most likely sound like baseball great Yogi Berra when he moved into his new digs in Montclair, New Jersey: "Wotta house. Nothin' but rooms!"

The ad for Leona's house leaves several unanswered questions. For example, we know about the bathrooms, but are there bedrooms? Does the kitchen have a dishwasher and garbage disposal system? Does the roof leak? Is the house wired for cable TV? Most importantly, does the house come with a 1,000-year contract? Perhaps this is one of those situations when, if you have to ask, you can't afford it.

However, we needn't ask, "Are the neighbors friendly?" In a world where it's tough to keep up with the neighbors, just think how tough it would be for the neighbors, the new owners of Leona's house, to stay ahead. Keeping up with the Joneses would be much less stressful than being the Joneses.

Imagine walking over to a neighbor's relatively squalid $5 million house and trying to borrow a cup of sugar. The ridicule and cold reception might prove to be unbearable.

"What? You want to borrow a cup of sugar? You live in the big $25 million house. Why don't you go out and buy a sugar beet farm?"

Not even Groucho Marx would have been impressed with Helmsley's house. According to one story about the popular comedian, he was reluctant to buy a showy house, but he finally succumbed to the pleadings of a realtor who wanted to show him a palatial ocean-front estate which was for sale.

The salesman drove the comedian up the mile-long, beautifully landscaped approach, escorted him through the house, the stables, the gardens and the kennels, all the while babbling of the wonders of this dream palace by the sea. Finally Groucho was ushered out on the flagged terrace and the realtor waved proudly toward the broad expanse of the Pacific.

"Now what do you think?" challenged the salesman.

"I don't care for it," replied Groucho. "Take away the ocean and what have you got?"

Take away the 36-foot waterfall and what have you got, Leona?

The Associated Press Vendetta

In a speech at the annual dinner of the Associated Press 92 years ago, Mark Twain talked eloquently about his hosts.

"There are only two forces that can carry light to all the corners of the globe," he declared, "the sun in the heavens and the Associated Press."

A person might say almost anything when there's a good meal at stake, but it must have bothered the AP to share honors with a celestial body. According to a headline released by the news service last month, "Hubble photos of dying stars give preview of sun's ultimate fate."

The accompanying article described how the Hubble Space Telescope photos give a preview of what ultimately will happen to the sun and how the Earth may be burnt to a crisp in about 6 billion years. What's good news for the AP is definitely bad news for the rest of us.

As it announced the pending demise of its greatest rival, the news service waxed poetically about what is expected to happen in the year 6,000,001,998.

"The sun will expand by about 200 times, searing the Earth to boiling temperatures. After a few thousand years, the sun will then collapse into a cooling white dwarf, its heat slowly diminishing."

Although the only remnants left from this century at that time will be Christmas fruitcakes and countless credit card balances, the news is still unsettling.

In its excitement, the AP fails to realize that our winning choice would have been the sun. Many manufacturers and vendors depend upon the sun for their livelihood. In fact, a sun power outage would make the current Asian economic crisis look like a bad hair day.

The AP hasn't taken into consideration that the demise of the sun will have an adverse effect upon the people who manufacture venetian blinds, car window visors, sunglasses, tanning and sunscreen products, solar heating panels and those decorative glass suncatchers, which often resemble colorful butterflies. None of those products would be needed in a sunless world.

While it tells the world that the sun, its greatest rival, is destined for doom, the AP should be asked, what good is it to report this type of news? It's much too apocalyptic for most of us to handle or solve.

It's one thing to neuter our pets when we read that the world has an overpopulation of dogs and cats or to floss our teeth when we hear on the TV news that dental problems are on the rise. It's quite another problem to know that our long-off descendants will face instant vaporization, an irresolvable dilemma.

In a cable from London to the Associated Press on June 2, 1897, Mark Twain noted, "The report of my death was an exaggeration." We can only hope that the same news service has exaggerated its report about the sun, our favorite star.

Bad Advice From Our Elders

"The trouble with most folks ain't so much their ignorance as knowing so many things that ain't so." Those words by Josh Billings make even more sense when we consider the great snowflake myth, which was debunked in the late 1980s.

After generations of children were raised on the winter maxim, "No two snowflakes are alike", scientists finally found two snowflakes with no discernable differences. According to a recent newspaper article, "The identiflakes were collected on an oil-coated glass slide dangling from a research plane flying over Wisconsin. The photographic proof is preserved at the National Center for Atmospheric Research in Boulder, Colorado."

Now that the snowflake theory has gone the way of Santa Claus and the tooth fairy, this might be a good time to review the other disproved claims which have been passed on from one generation to another:

"When boys grow up they only marry nice girls."

"If you cross your eyes, they will stay crossed and no surgeon in the country will be able to straighten them."

"If you eat candy all of your teeth will fall out."

"Don't swallow chewing gum because it will never leave your body."

"If you pull out a grey hair, two more will grow in its place."

"You have to clean your plate because children are starving in Africa."

"If your underwear is less than satisfactory and you are involved in an accident, you will become the main topic of conversation in the hospital emergency room."

"If you step on a sidewalk crack, you will break your mother's back."

"If you crack your knuckles they will double in size."

"Cover a burn with butter."

"Don't go near the water after eating."

"Patent-leather shoes and mud puddles reflect up your skirt."

"If you don't take six years of math you will be a miserable failure for the rest of your life." ("And," my geometry teacher reasoned, "you will never be able to divide a recipe.")

"Of course I know what you're doing — I have eyes in the back of my head."

"Be careful what you say because the walls have ears."

"If you open that umbrella in the house, one of us is going to die."

In hushed tones a home economics teacher told my sister, "Red knee-socks will increase a young man's ardor."

Several years before, a fourth grade teacher told my class, "If you sleep on your left side, your heart many stop beating."

"Spanking you like this hurts me more than it hurts you."

These are only examples of the wisdom that helped shape our lives. When as children we accepted everything we heard as the gospel truth, we didn't know about George Bernard Shaw who wrote, "Beware of false knowledge; it is more dangerous than ignorance."

By telling us that no two snowflakes are alike, our elders wanted us to know that each of us was special and unique. Now that the truth is out, it's comforting to know there are other flakes like us around.

Bad Mouthing The Food On Our Tables

We should think twice before we discredit carrots, disparage pears or deride rutabagas. Thirteen states, reacting to pressure from agricultural groups, have already adopted food defamation laws and more than a dozen others are considering similar legislation.

The statutes make it possible for farmers and ranchers to sue consumer groups, health advocates, journalists or anyone else who spreads false information about the safety of a food product.

Two troubling questions are raised by the new laws. Are we the "anyone else"? What will happen if the laws are carried to an extreme and also apply to personal opinions about certain food products?

During his term in office, former President George Bush admitted his disdain for broccoli. Under the new laws, could he have been impeached? On the other hand, he might been been reprieved in light of his favorable comments about pork rinds.

The statutes' first court test took place this year with ranchers claiming that TV talk show hostess Oprah Winfrey and a guest bad-mouthed beef in 1996. At one point during the program, Winfrey announced that she would stop eating hamburgers. In the end, the ranchers failed after they demanded $6.7 million in damages from Winfrey, her guest and her production company.

When the new laws have more teeth and more people are taken to court, and when people subsequently refuse to sink their teeth into certain food products, we may expect to see a magazine article entitled, "Why

Johnny Went to Jail".

The article will describe how Johnny and his mother spent their last meal together at a local restaurant.

"But, Mom, I hate..."

"Shhh, Johnny! Eat the food on your pla..."

"But I hate..."

"Don't say it, Johnny!"

"But I HATE CARROTS!"

At this point, a seemingly mild-mannered man, who had been dining inconspicuously at a nearby table, walked over to their table and flashed his Veggie Task Force badge.

"I'm sorry, ma'am, but we'll have to take your son in for questioning."

"But...but...he's only twelve years old!"

"So was Billy the Kid at one time, ma'am. At least Billy had one thing going for him — he didn't bad mouth the entire carrot industry."

Similar heart-wrenching scenes will be played over much of our country if the new laws, referred to as "banana bills" and "veggie libel" by their opponents, go into effect and are enforced.

Most Americans have nothing against leafy, green and yellow vegetables. On countless occasions we have taken them into our homes for dinners. However, when it comes to certain foods — such as lima beans or salmon loaf — we must stand up for our freedom of expression and proclaim, "Lettuce alone!"

On a personal note, I would like to take this opportunity to apologize to asparagus growers everywhere. I was only kidding when I told everyone that I hated eating your product. Honestly, just kidding.

The Scrabble Competition

It's the "come hither" look I know so well. It's evening and the arching of his eyebrows suggests, "Shall we?"

My eyes flutter back the subtle message, "Why not?"

We refer, of course, to playing Scrabble.

The popular board game is celebrating its 50th anniversary this year. According to the Des Moines Register, "When he began amusing himself with a tactile crossword puzzle, Alfred Butts had no illusions of fame or fortune. It was the Depression, he was unemployed, and what better to do in 1931 than to while away the empty days inventing a board game?" The game went public in 1948.

What better way indeed. What better way to pit brother against brother, sister against sister or mother against father? While the Civil War had served much the same purpose, Butts found a neater substitute. Instead of having uniformed bodies splayed about the ground, egos, senses of self-esteem and even marital harmony could be silently obliterated.

Somewhere between dallying with secretaries and forgetting wedding anniversaries, you might find another cause for marital discord — the game called Scrabble. In our home the game is a wintertime activity, a concession to the fact that it's too cold for us to compete on the golf course.

Our addiction to the game began in 1962, shortly

after we were married, and it continues to this day. During one early game, my husband had been blessed with a wealth of consonants, including Q (worth 10 points) and X (8 points). At the same time, I was suffering from an irregularity which often affects Scrabble players — the inability to move my vowels.

It wasn't a pretty picture and after his dubious victory I refused to speak to him for two days. Unfortunately we didn't mellow out over the years. While they were growing up, the mere mention of a Scrabble game between their parents would send our children fleeing to their rooms. Their earlier concerns about whether we would eventually separate after a particularly heated game have dwindled somewhat and we no longer have to allay their fears. After all, they're in their 30s now and they're living quite independently in far-off states. They no longer have to decide which parent will become their primary guardian.

Admittedly, the game has been taken to an extreme in our home. What else could explain my compulsion to add up word points on billboards and backs of cereal boxes? Charles Lamb apparently foresaw the pitfalls of Scrabble when he wrote, "Man is a gaming animal. He must always try to get the better in something or other."

And life must have been treating him very well when Grantland Rice noted, "It doesn't matter whether you win or lose, but how you play the game." Obviously, Mr. Rice never played Scrabble during a long Midwestern winter.

Judging from his optimism, he would have been the player with most of the valuable consonants.

Hobbledehoy Names

William Shakespeare's question, "What's in a name?" may soon take on new dimensions.

A recent article in the Washington Post described how Brande Stellings and David Soskin, two newly-married, Ivy League-educated lawyers in New York City, gave new meaning to the expression "name calling". In their wedding announcement on the New York Times society page, one sentence read, "Mr. Soskin will take Ms. Stellings's surname."

In the United States, where only 10 percent of married women are keeping their maiden names, combining last names (as in the case of Hillary Rodham Clinton), or doing creative things with hyphens, the New York couple has set a new precedent.

The Washington Post article also noted that there is no equivalent term for "maiden name". For the sake of argument, I would suggest "boyhood name" or "hobbledehoy name", with the latter referring to any boy or adolescent youth. Actually, "hobbledehoy" balances quite nicely with "maiden", a term reserved for a girl or a young unmarried woman.

Future application and income tax forms could easily accommodate the expression, "maiden or hobbledehoy name".

David Stellings, the new groom, noted that his friends were surprised with the name change. He observed, "They warned that it would be really annoying, having to change my credit cards, change my business cards. How would people who knew me before find me?" The implication of their concerns is that females somehow enjoy the confusion of changing their names and losing their identities after they are married.

If this new name-change option would have been available when our country was founded, our national monuments, forefathers, and businesses would reflect the surnames of not-so-famous wives. For example, would we be able to recognize the monuments in our nation's capitol dedicated to the memory of Thomas Skelton, George Custis and Abraham Todd? The carved faces at Mount Rushmore would belong to Skelton, Custis, Todd and that well-known rough rider, Teddy Lee Carow.

If Christopher Columbus would have taken the surname of his wife, de Perestrello, CBS (the Columbia Broadcasting System) would have become PBS, and we would have de Perestrello University in New York, the de Perestrello River in the Northwest and several cities and towns with different names.

"The Tell-Tale Heart" and "The Raven" would have been written by Edgar Allan Clemm.

Sir Winston Hozier would have proclaimed, "I have nothing to offer but blood, toil, tears and sweat."

Our post-World War II presidents would have included Harry Wallace, Dwight Doud, John Bouvier, Lyndon Taylor, Richard Ryan, Gerald Bloomer, Jimmy Smith, Ronald Robbins and George Pierce.

The only president who would have escaped the name change problem was Franklin Delano Roosevelt. He had all the bases covered when he married his fourth cousin, Eleanor Roosevelt.

Finally, we will never forget William Hathaway, the famous bard of England who wrote, "What's in a name?" His hobbledehoy name was Shakespeare.

Advice For New Parents

If everything goes according to plan, my husband and I will become grandparents for the first time in May. In a flurry of unbridled excitement we suddenly find ourselves buying tiny baby garments, cutting down golf clubs to fit a toddler's grip and examining our faces for new wrinkles.

Except for the advice thing, we have accepted the news quite well. When our daughter and son-in-law phoned most recently, informing us that the new baby was indeed a boy, she closed the conversation with a surprising statement, "I'll be calling you for advice."

In all honesty I've forgotten what it's like to have a baby in the house. When we last held a newborn baby in our arms, Richard Nixon and Spiro Agnew were still in the White House and all of our clothes were 100 percent polyester. Fathers were spared from the harsher realities of life going on in the delivery rooms. A rumor, surely too good to be true, was circulating about a new product on the market — disposable diapers.

However, after doing some reading and talking with other grandparents, I'm ready to dispense some solicited advice. That in itself will be a new experience. "Unsolicited" and "advice" have been our operative words as parents for the past 31 years.

The following advice would apply to any new parents-to-be:

Children are born with self-destructive tendencies. They are capable of putting anything smaller than a basketball in their mouths. The best way to prepare for this stage in your child's development would be to tune in "Wild Kingdom" reruns and watch snakes devour small animals in a single gulp.

Expect messes. Imogene Fey once noted, "You will know what is meant by a spitting image when you try to feed cereal to a baby."

Don't worry about cleaning the house for the next few decades. It will resume its lived-in look before the vacuum cleaner is back in the closet. Along those same lines, never allow your children to write the date on dusty furniture.

Understand the roles of your parents as you bring a new life into the world. Grandparents are people who come to your house, spoil the children, and then go home.

You should expect to give up certain luxuries after the baby is born, such as shampooing your hair, leisurely grocery shopping and brushing your teeth.

Send out thank-you notes for baby gifts before your child reaches "the terrible twos." At that time your handwriting will become illegible and you will develop incoherent speech patterns. You will be speaking in monosyllables.

Avoid saying "My child would never do such and such" because in a short time they will do it. By the time the words, "My child is potty-trained", have left your lips, that same child will be standing in a warm puddle.

Until their selective hearing problems are adjusted later, babies and small children cannot understand the word "no." In many cases, this selective hearing is carried into adulthood.

Get used to saying, "It's not the gift, it's the thought

that counts", until your baby is 35 or 40, at which time you will be able to show your materialistic side. After all, it's possible for a household to have too many refrigerator magnets and bird feeders made from plastic milk jugs. Feel free to think in terms of large-screen TVs, updated computer systems or extended vacations in Hawaii.

Establish guilt patterns as soon as the baby is born. All of his admirable traits should be linked to the people who provided you with an orthodontist, piano lessons and prom dresses. Less desirable traits should be attributed to the other side of the family.

Having children opens the door to joyous chaos. Once that door is opened there will be no going back to the way things used to be.

Perhaps the best observation about parenthood came from actor Martin Mull, who knew about joyous chaos and noted, "Having a family is like having a bowling alley installed in your brain."

Carole Achterhof's four humor books may be ordered through:

Bare Bones Books
Rural Route 9061
Spirit Lake, IA 51360

The following order form may be photocopied.

Please rush____copies of HE'S A KEEPER, I'M A TOSSER____copies of LIFE WITH A CHANNEL SURFER,____copies of POTATO CHIPS ARE VEGETABLES and/or____copies of NEVER TRUST A SIZE THREE at $9.95 each.
(An additional $2.00 for postage and handling is required for orders of 1-4 books.)

Enclosed is my check or money order for $_____, payable to BARE BONES BOOKS.

NAME_____

STREET _____

CITY _____STATE ____ZIP_____